# The Squire of
# Warm Springs

By Theo Lippman, Jr.

THE SQUIRE OF WARM SPRINGS
SENATOR TED KENNEDY
SPIRO AGNEW'S AMERICA
MUSKIE (with Donald C. Hansen)
A GANG OF PECKSNIFFS by H. L. Mencken (Editor)

# The Squire of Warm Springs

### F.D.R. IN GEORGIA 1924-1945

## by Theo Lippman, Jr.

ᑫᑲP  *A Playboy Press Book*

FIRST EDITION

Playboy and Rabbit Head design are trademarks of Playboy, 919 North Michigan Avenue, Chicago, Illinois 60611 (U.S.A.), reg. U.S. Pat., marca registrada, marque déposée.

Trade distribution by Simon and Schuster
A Division of Gulf + Western Corporation
New York, New York 10020

ISBN: 0-671-16967-X

Library of Congress Cataloging in Publication Data

Lippman, Theo.
    The squire of Warm Springs.
    Includes bibliographical references and index.
    1. Roosevelt, Franklin Delano, Pres., U. S., 1882-
1945.  2. Warm Springs, Ga.—History.  3. United
States—Economic policy—1933-1945.  4. Physically
handicapped—United States.  5. Presidents—United
States—Biography.  I. Title.
E807.L58      973.917'092'4 [B]      77-13016

For Laura

# Contents

# The Squire of
# Warm Springs

# Preface: "From Peanuts to Politics"

Why another book about Franklin Roosevelt? There are five reasons for this one. One is plain, simple nostalgia on the part of the author. I grew up in Georgia in the 1930s and 1940s in an environment in which Roosevelt was worshiped. It was not just that family and friends benefited from New Deal measures or that Roosevelt's leadership gave us the courage and optimism required in the depths of the Depression. It was also that he made us in Georgia a part of the nation in a way that our local politicians never did. In fact, our local politicians did just the opposite. They glorified our separateness, insisted that it would always be that way. This was most directly related to the racial issue, but in other subtle and not-so-subtle ways Georgians (and Alabamans and Mississippians) were always being reminded that we were outside the mainstream of American life. That a Georgian could ever become a national leader was not only unspoken but unthought. Even in 1977 it is hard to believe that it could come to pass. To

3

the extent that he was a Georgian, Roosevelt made our American-ness whole.

A second reason for another look at Roosevelt in this sort of book is that there is a national nostalgia for simpler times. Many Americans probably don't even believe that Presidents ever lived simple lives in simple surroundings, amid ordinary people, without the emblems and accessories of the so-called Imperial Presidency interfering to the point of obliterating any honest, direct links between the people and the President. Although Roosevelt *created* the Imperial Presidency, his life—particularly at Warm Springs—shows that a President does not have to give in to it, does not have to be a prisoner of it. The modern presidency is all-powerful, but it is not that all-powerful, and it does not require either a moving wall of security to deprive the people of their President (and vice versa) or a life-style exalted (à la Hyannisport, San Clemente, and so forth) to the point that the people-President link of common experience is ruptured.

A third reason for this book is to remind its readers that for all the importance of the Brain Trust, which is a short-hand way of saying available expert theoretical knowledge, the President who employed that also had firsthand knowledge of depressed rural life. He tempered the one with the other. The experts wrote the legislation, but a character in the real-life drama—Roosevelt—let the experts know what he had learned in living as well as in thinking.

A fourth reason is to try to recall that special-interest group Roosevelt was so much a captive of: the cripples of the earth, the companions of Warm Springs, particularly. "I am speaking to you tonight from Georgia Warm Springs Foundation for the victims of infantile paralysis," Roosevelt told a national audience via radio one day in 1940, "and I always feel that in this atmosphere one gets a better perspective of life, a better sense of proportion about all sorts of things, from peanuts to politics." It was a unique presidential perspective, and likely will always be. A man or woman with Roosevelt's disability would have, I believe, little chance of being elected President today.

Which brings me to the fifth and sixth reasons for this book. The fifth reason is that I believe one of the wellsprings of the New Deal and the rest of the achievements of the Roosevelt presidency was his humanity. The other sources were his intellect (which, despite some famous comments to the contrary, was first-rate, if by intellect we mean broad knowledge and the ability to comprehend it), his winning personality, his political astuteness, his ability to select and draw the best from a wide variety of assistants. I believe his humanity is seen in boldest relief in Warm Springs, and owes much of its development to his lameness.

The seventh reason for this book is to remind the public and my colleagues in the press that the relationship between journalists and Presidents that has dominated the past decade—one of mutual distrust and dislike—is not the way it has to be. Perhaps the press corps of the 1930s and 1940s was too considerate of Roosevelt's privacy. Perhaps not. At any rate, the fact that reporters of that day kept their attention focused on issues and politics and statecraft is, it seems to me, worth pondering. It was not just Roosevelt's legs that the press ignored. It was also his involved relationship with his farm, with the Georgia Warm Springs Foundation and with the National Foundation. There were all sorts of conflicts of interest. The Georgia Warm Springs Foundation bought him a car. Friends of his got special treatment there. An adviser moved back and forth from government project to farm to foundation—often wearing several hats in the same day. That Roosevelt was allowed his several conflicting endeavors allowed him to continue to be a citizen while President. Today, there is a great call for—indeed a demand that—politicians be full-time politicians. Conflicts of interest are almost literally taboo. The citizen-leader is becoming a thing of the past. That is not at all a desirable thing, if Roosevelt's life is as relevant as I believe it still is, and I don't believe it has to be considered an inevitable thing.

I have tried to indicate as I went along where I got the material I was depending on. The Roosevelt literature is vast, and I have barely dipped a toe into it. But in addition to the works cited at the end of each chapter, these were used:

*The Formative Years of Social Security*, by Arthur J. Altmeyer; *Roosevelt: The Lion and the Fox*, by James MacGregor Burns; *I Write from Washington*, by Marquis Childs; *White House Witness*, by Jonathan Daniels; the Frank Freidel series referred to in a chapter note is, so far, four volumes: *The Apprenticeship, The Ordeal, The Triumph,* and *Launching the New Deal*; *When the New Deal Was Young and Gay*, by Charles Hurd; *The Secret Diary of Harold L. Ickes* (two volumes); *Eleanor and Franklin*, by Joseph Lash; *Franklin D. Roosevelt*, edited by William L. Leuchtenburg; *After Seven Years*, by Raymond Moley; *Roosevelt and Howe*, by Alfred Rollins, Jr.; *Roosevelt and Hopkins*, by Robert E. Sherwood; *The Age of Roosevelt* in three volumes (so far): *The Crisis of the Old Order,*

*The Coming of the New Deal,* and *The Politics of Upheaval,* by Arthur Schlesinger, Jr.; and *New Deal Thought,* edited by Howard Zinn. *Invincible Summer, an Intimate Portrait of the Roosevelts,* based on the recollections of Marion Dickerman, by Kenneth S. Davis, is both a memoir and a fine picture book. Two other useful picture books are *The Human Side of F.D.R.,* by Richard Harrity and Ralph G. Martin; and *FDR: A Pictorial Biography,* by Stefan Lorant.

A great deal of the material in this book is drawn from interviews conducted in Georgia, Washington, and, by telephone, elsewhere, in 1976 and 1977. I would like to thank all those who granted me the time. I can't name them all here, but I can and must name a few who were patient with me through repeated interviews and queries or who trusted me with memoirs or family souvenirs that were quite helpful. First are Joe and Margaret Thompson of Warm Springs, who supplied me with much data about the Georgia Warm Springs Foundation plus the marvelous manuscript of her father, the Reverend W. G. Harry. Mary Hudson Veeder was equally generous with her time and old photographs of the early days at Warm Springs. W. Tapley Bennett, Sr., granted me hours of reminiscences and answers to questions. So did Frank Allcorn, Jr. So did Mr. and Mrs. Fred Moore (Otis's son). I also want to thank Ann Irwin Bray, Mrs. Virginia Callaway, Mrs. Leonard Cochran, Mrs. Nelle Lee, Mr. and Mrs. Hoke Shipp, Mrs. Hoke Smith, Miss Virginia Pond, Mrs. W. B. Persons, Mrs. Eugene Brown, Sr., Dr. and Mrs. Stuart Raper, Margaret Ross, Mrs. Adah Toombs, Joe Young, Mrs. Robert Rainey, Betty Brown and Mildred Reed. I know I have carelessly left some names off this list and I apologize. The reason I was able to talk to so many Georgians is that Celestine Sibley wrote a column in the Atlanta *Journal-Constitution* about my plans to do a book like this. I was inundated by letters from people volunteering to talk to me or—equally gracious—recommending that I get in touch with some friend. This experience certainly reinforced my beliefs in southern hospitality and the power of the press—or, at least, the influence of so fine and respected a journalist as my friend Celestine Sibley.

Finally, there are the professionals who helped me so much in this project. Director William Emerson and his staff at the Franklin D. Roosevelt Library in Hyde Park were helpful beyond the call of duty in this case, since the author is a journalist who was embarking for the first time on a historical project. Other archivists and librarians who have provided valuable assistance are those at the Little White House and Museum, the National Archives (particularly in the newsreel and still-picture divisions), the Georgia Archives, the Atlanta Historical Society, the Library of Congress, the *Sunpapers*, Johns Hopkins University and the Johns Hopkins Medical School and the Enoch Pratt Free Library. Last and not least is Madeline Lippman. Her training is in children's literature and libraries, but she quickly learned her way around the Roosevelt Library and spent two vacations and a weekend there going through the thousands of items that were or could have been related to this book.

The author alone is responsible for errors, and hopes that readers will call them to his attention so that corrections can be made.

# The Last Thanksgiving

---

Thanksgiving came late to Warm Springs, Georgia, in 1944. A great war was on and the American Commander in Chief, President Franklin D. Roosevelt, had been delayed 5 days in coming down. He had founded the tradition of celebrating Thanksgiving there with dinner and a speech for the patients and staff of the health spa in the little Georgia town nearly two decades ago. The traditional turkey dinner and speech became a casualty of war in 1942. So when the President told his friends in Warm Springs that he could make the trip in 1944 but would be late, they enthusiastically agreed to postpone their Thanksgiving celebration. Now, on the Tuesday evening of Nov. 28, Roosevelt began to speak, a rambling recollection of Thanksgivings past. He remained seated in a straight-backed chair. Many in his audience were seated in wheelchairs. Like the speaker, they were victims of one of the most dread and certainly one of the most publicized diseases of the era before 1955—infantile paralysis or poliomyelitis. It was caused by an unknown agent, struck whole communities, left its victims with crippled limbs or lungs. Roosevelt spoke about the history of the effort, led by him, to conquer that disease. He had come over 21 years before to the little Georgia community of Warm Springs and the institution where now he spoke, then in the fourth year of a search for a cure for himself, unable to walk unaided since polio had struck him down in 1921. His search up and down the Eastern Seaboard for a cure had been futile.

He recalled some of that in his Thanksgiving remarks. Occasionally, he would lose the thread of his narrative and turn to the subject of the great war effort he, as Commander in Chief, was leading. Then he would catch himself and reminisce again about the early days at Warm Springs.

He had bought the place, then a resort, in 1927, and turned it into a world-famous center for the study of polio and after-care for its victims. The institution he had founded was always special to Roosevelt. He had found after becoming President that he could relax more in the little Georgia backwater than he could anyplace else. He built a house there and bought a farm. And the progress the Georgia Warm Springs Foundation and its offspring, the National Foundation for Infantile Paralysis, were to make was more of a satisfaction to him in the field of social achievement than anything he accomplished as a government leader, with the one possible exception of the Social Security Administration. In the midst of history's greatest war, one burdensome to the President beyond comparison, he had found time to keep informed about the smallest detail at Warm Springs. In the previous year he had requested a report on a poignant case involving the daughter of a serviceman. He sent some murder mysteries to the foundation's small library. He inquired of a retired foundation official about his new life on a Georgia farm. He exchanged letters and memos concerning a memorial for the man who had tried and failed to make a go of the old resort that Roosevelt had turned into the foundation. He interceded with his farm operator to get more fresh food to the foundation, and he apparently interceded with a government agency when bureaucratic red tape ensnarled it. The simplest things came to his attention; his confidential secretaries knew he wanted them to. The previous March, for example, a secretary brought to him, along with his usual mountain of wartime, election-year material, a letter from "Warm Springs Kids" (the only signature) requesting that the foundation's pool, open to the public, not be closed, as it was expected to be. The "Kids" said the next-nearest pool was 12 miles away, a long trip in a year in which gasoline was rationed. FDR dashed off a memorandum to Basil O'Connor, his former law partner, whom he had pressured into taking over first the Georgia Warm Springs Foundation and then the National Foundation. "Doc, [he said] . . . as you know, I am a crank on keeping the pool open. I wonder if we could do it on a concession basis. I think that two able-bodied women could do it!"

Doc was at the head table now. In the language of the afflicted, he was "able-bodied." That is, he was not a "polio." Another able-bodied member at the Thanksgiving Dinner speech was Leighton McCarthy. He was retiring as Canadian ambassador to the United States. He and Roosevelt were long-time Warm Springs friends. McCarthy's son John was a polio. Both McCarthy and O'Connor must have been thinking about past Thanksgiving dinners as the

President rambled. Roosevelt had carved his first Warm Springs turkey at what he dubbed Founder's Day on Thanksgiving, 1928. That gala celebration was in honor of one of the foundation's first great steps forward under his stewardship. The old primitive pools where the curative natural warm waters that gushed from under Pine Mountain were gathered for play and for healing were added to that year by a handsome glass-enclosed pool. Therapy could continue into the short but occasionally bitter winters of southwest Georgia. 1928 was a pleasanter year than 1944. There was a sense of beginning in 1928. There was a sense of ending in 1944. The fight against the disease was nearer victory than anyone there knew. But 1944 had been a bad year. There were over 18,000 cases in that year's epidemic, the most in America since 1916.

In 1928, Franklin Roosevelt had just been elected governor of New York. Some of his Georgia neighbors were already promoting him for President. Despite his infirmity, Roosevelt was the very picture of a virile, robust and healthy man. He had developed powerful chest and arm muscles from his therapeutic swimming and other exercises. He carried some 190 pounds on his six-foot-plus frame. He looked heavier and would have been if his legs were not withered. He glowed with an autumn tan acquired in three weeks of rest and relaxation following the New York election. His spirits were high. After an evening of fun and games and mischievous speeches and skits, the 46-year-old Founder would lead one team in a water football game in the new pool. The game was played with a sponge wrapped in oilskin. Six players on a side. The object was to get the sponge from one end of the pool to the other. Roosevelt predicted victory as he delivered that first

Founder's Day speech. He was wrong, it turned out. He and a team of other patients lost 12-0 to a team of women physiotherapists.

Now, on November 28, 1944, the tanned Roosevelt of 1928 had been replaced by a gray and somewhat stooped man with deep circles under his eyes. His weight had begun to fall earlier in the year and was now down to 160. He had heart disease. He looked worse than he was, with wattles hanging under the famous chin, but he wasn't well by any stretch. For a while his doctor, a young Navy cardiologist named Howard Bruenn, had had to order him to stop his still-favorite pastime, swimming. He had put him on a special diet, so he'd gain some weight. Bruenn also thought Roosevelt's lazing in the sun would help his looks and his morale. The trip to Warm Springs was part of a plan to help the tired President recover some vigor. The war and the tough fourth-term campaign had sapped his strength. The war had interrupted his visits. In 1944 he was back in Warm Springs for the first Thanksgiving vacation since 1939.

In 1941, the President had come for a visit on November 28 and left after one day. War was imminent. His secretary and friend Grace Tully, who accompanied him on his Georgia trips, said that one day's visit was the last one in which the President was in a "holiday and carefree mood."

But it would be a mistake to think that all gaiety had been driven from Warm Springs by the war. War's glamour and excitement could be as palpable in hospitals as in other theaters. Bette Davis, the movie actress, had come over from a nearby Army installation to join the President at dinner. Doc O'Connor and White House staff members were dismayed, but could not prevent her from sitting next to the

13

President for most of the evening. Several Navy men were in the audience that night, resplendent in immaculate uniforms; many, like so many of the children, were in wheelchairs. Georgia Hall's dining room was long and narrow, with windows on the two long sides. The tables with their white linen were arranged so that wheelchairs could roll comfortably close and still leave aisles for the waiters. But an accident occurred. A waiter dropped a tray of dirty dishes on the head, shoulders and lap of a Navy officer. His fellow officers and a few enlisted men began to giggle, then laugh. For the newcomers, at least, the evening was as magical in 1944 as it was in 1928. They were seeing the President for the first time, with no memories of a healthier man to compare to the pale Commander in Chief. He looked all right to them.

The skit of the evening was also gay. The program was called "The Spirit of Warm Springs." It was dedicated to Franklin D. Roosevelt. There was a depiction of "The Past." Then, "The Present." In the latter, much was made of the existence of "the gobs" at the new facility the Navy had established at the foundation. As a special treat for the President, so recently victorious at the polls, two of the members of the staff came out in a Democratic donkey suit to dance for him. Then the whole crowd had sung such traditional songfest numbers as "I've Been Workin' on the Railroad." They also sang a slightly modified current popular hit: "Oh, Mr. Roosevelt/ Come out and play with me/ And bring your dollies three/ Climb up my apple tree. . . ." Nowhere was pomp and imperial manner less evident in Roosevelt and in his audience than at the Georgia Warm Springs Foundation. To the end, to the young polios, if not to the able-bodied, he was "Uncle Rosey."

There was a tradition within the tradition of Founder's Day dinners. The Founder would stand at the door after the meal and the skits and the speech and shake hands with each departing patient and staff member. In the '20s and '30s, Roosevelt could stand for extended periods of time with both his legs locked tightly in metal and leather braces, and with a cane or strong arm to lean on. It was painful, but he could do it. By the end of the '30s, Roosevelt was wearing his braces less and less—and so standing less and less. So he sat in his wheelchair with Miss Alice Plastridge at his side to shake hands with each departing guest that November. Miss Plastridge had come to the Foundation in 1927 to assist the lone doctor and lone physiotherapist at the institution. She remained to become the chief physiotherapist. The gray President grasped each proffered hand and said a few words. If he was preoccupied or overly tired, he did not show it. In fact, 20 or 30 years later, several people who were there that night could not recall that he was not a well man. One guest, an adult in 1944, recalled vividly that he *stood* to shake her hand. He could not have. Another guest who was barely in her teens remembered only how impressive Roosevelt looked, how warm and strong his hands were as he clasped hers in friendly greeting.

There were exceptions. Fred Botts was a polio himself and one of the very first Warm Springs patients after Roosevelt. He had remained as a business official of the foundation. He portrayed a new patient in that evening's skit. He winced at the sight of his old friend. When Roosevelt coughed, he turned away, unable to look.

Roosevelt had arrived in Georgia only a day before this, his last, Founder's Day Dinner; he stayed there for two and a half more weeks. It was as pure a vacation as he could expect in the middle of a war. A pouch of important business came by courier from Washington every day. He dozed in the sun on the porch of the Little White House, saw his old love, Lucy Rutherfurd, who stayed in the nearby guest house the first week of his vacation there. He swam for the first time the week after she left for her home in South Carolina. His blood pressure soared (260/250 mm Hg), so Doctor Bruenn discouraged further dips.

A large crowd of townsfolk came to see Roosevelt off, as usual. Some had become close friends, either through his farm or the foundation. Some were just associates. Some he knew only casually or not at all. But he was a hero and more to the plain people of Meriwether and surrounding counties. He was a political hero and something more. The first Roosevelt for President Club was formed in Meriwether County in 1930 by Dr. R. D. Gilbert. Even before that a county newspaper's owner, Judge Henry Revill, had endorsed such a candidacy. He named the Little White House that before the 1928 election. FDR had received his first 21-gun salute in Warm Springs—21 giant firecrackers exploded for him on his Thanksgiving visit of 1932 by the Georgia Warm Springs Foundation's auditor, Ben S. Purse. Some among his Georgia following approached with reverential feelings. He always enjoyed political popularity there, far more so than in Dutchess County, New York. His greatest victories—and one of his greatest defeats—were registered in Meriwether County. He said his good-byes at the little train station, promising to be back as soon as possible.

His appearance had improved in his three-week visit. He had regained his color. His Georgia friends felt better about him, and reasonably expected to see him back. And, in fact, he did come back, sooner than they expected. In a little over three months, he returned to Warm Springs to spend the last two weeks of his life there.

## *A note on sources for this chapter*

Much of this information came from interviews with people who were in Warm Springs in 1944 and earlier. I also drew on newspaper accounts in the *New York Times,* and, to a lesser degree, the *Warm Springs Mirror.* In this and in every chapter, I have used a draft document prepared by Rexford G. Tugwell for the Roosevelt Warm Springs Memorial Commission, entitled "Franklin D. Roosevelt at Warm Springs, Georgia/Some Chronological Landmarks." Among books, *FDR's Last Year* by Jim Bishop is good. So is *Off the Record with FDR* by William D. Hassett. Dr. Howard G. Bruenn's "Clinical Notes of the Illness and Death of President Franklin D. Roosevelt" is most helpful. It appeared in the April 1970 issue of *Annals of Internal Medicine.* There are memoranda in several files at the Roosevelt Library at Hyde Park relating to the President's Georgia sojourns. There is no record of his remarks at the November 30 dinner. A copy of the 1944 program, as well as a personal written memoir of the event, were provided me by Mrs. Mildred Lee Reed, who was a part-time worker at the foundation while attending high school. She was a most attentive watcher that night.

# *Before Warm Springs*

Poliomyelitis is an age-old disease. Scientists have found that it existed in the pre-Christian era. But the first written records of this disease that attacks the brain and spinal cord, that hits children more often than adults, that usually occurs in epidemics, and that leaves between half and three-quarters of its victims with some degree of leg, arm or trunk paralysis and thereafter with withered and strengthless muscles (and is even fatal in many cases) appeared in 1835 in Britain. Several epidemics occurred there, and in the United States in the nineteenth century. The disease is caused by a virus so small that its discovery did not come until the first decade of this century, when it was also first proved in a laboratory that the disease is infectious. In 1916 the disease first broke through into the American public's consciousness and became a dreaded scourge. In that year, the 20 states that kept records of infectious diseases reported 27,367 cases and 7,179 deaths. In New York City alone there were 9,023 cases and 2,448 deaths. One student of that epidemic estimates that, when unreported very mild cases of polio are taken into account, it is likely that almost every New York family was affected by the 1916 outbreak.

Polio was, in the first part of the twentieth century, mostly a disease of the middle classes. The virus is found in untreated sewage. The usual infection comes from unclean food or water, introduced into the body through the nose or mouth. The very poor commonly came into contact with the virus as infants in their unsanitary slums. At that stage of muscular development, the virus's assault on the brain and nervous system did no damage. It did, however, give the infant a lifetime immunity to polio. Franklin Roosevelt, even more than the average member of his class, was shielded from the infectious diseases of infancy and early childhood. His childhood diseases came late. He had scarlet fever at 14, mumps and measles at 16, probably because he didn't start school until late.

Roosevelt was the sort of individual for whom a crippling disease represented a special tragedy. Although he was never an outstanding athlete—he was cut from the freshman football team at Harvard—he was an enormously energetic and physically active individual. He liked to swim, iceboat, sail, fish, ride, play tennis and golf. He even liked calisthenics. Even more to the point, in his professional life he like to *go*, to see firsthand and close up the people and problems he had to deal with. His whole personality seemed to depend on that movement, that energy. It was central to what is now called "image." "He would leap over a rail rather than open a gate," one of his sons said of him. There is a picture of him in the National Archives as Assistant Secretary of the Navy that shows as well as anything what polio claimed. FDR is shown, dapper and slim, aloft in the rigging of a ship on an inspection tour. You look at that picture and think that to take away that man's legs would be an ironic punishment of Greek, almost Biblical, intensity. Yet he overcame that blow, denied it, actually, and convinced the world to do the same.

The story of the attack is a well-known bit of American lore. It took place at the family retreat on Campobello Island off the coast of Maine, where Franklin Roosevelt had spent summers since 1883, the year after he was born. But as an adult, his stays were often brief. The family had gone without him in 1916, during the polio scare. Franklin Jr. had been born there in 1914. In 1921, after eight busy years in Washington, Roosevelt was able to get away for an extended vacation at Campobello for the first time in nearly a decade. His aide and political adviser, Louis Howe, was also going to vacation there. Roosevelt thought he himself would run for governor of New York in 1922. He had become a nationally known Democratic leader in 1920, when he was his party's vice presidential nominee on the losing James M. Cox ticket. He could even reasonably dream and plan on a presidential nomination in 1924, though he would be only 42 years old, and though no wealthy aristocrat had won the Democratic party's presidential nomination in modern times.

Roosevelt joined his family at Campobello at the beginning of August after a yacht trip up with the Baltimore financier and publisher Van Lear Black. He threw himself into the vigors of a Rooseveltian vacation, though he said once he could not shake the feeling of tiredness he had brought with him. On August 10 he spent a particularly wearying day, sailing, fighting a brush fire, taking two swims. The next morning he had trouble getting out of bed. Soon he had a fever of 102° and weakness and paralysis in arms and legs. Dr. Eben Bennett, the physician from nearby Lubec who had delivered Franklin Jr., thought it was just a cold. When, on the following day, Roosevelt could not stand, Eleanor sent Louis Howe and Dr. Bennett to find a specialist in one of the many nearby vacation resorts. They found Dr. W. W. Keen of Philadelphia. He examined Roosevelt, diagnosed his malady as a blood clot in the lower spinal cord. He recommended vigorous massage, which was exactly the wrong treatment for polio-affected muscles at that early stage. Later, he sent a bill for $600, a shock at which Eleanor often expressed outrage later.

Unsatisfied with Keen's diagnosis, the family tracked down another renowned specialist, Dr. Robert Lovett, a Boston orthopedist. He came to Campobello on August 25, and immediately diagnosed polio. Both he and Dr. Bennett told Roosevelt he would recover. Dr. Lovett's prognosis was, in retrospect, a cautious one, to the effect that if Roosevelt's will to be active was strong enough, he should regain the use of his legs. To the Roosevelts, at the time, the words must have seemed more optimistic than the doctor intended. Dr. Bennett was more optimistic still, promising the family and Roosevelt that he would "be all right." Dr. Lovett recommended that Roosevelt go to a hospital for further diagnosis and treatment. On September 13, a month after he was stricken, Roosevelt left Campobello Island for New York City's Presbyterian Hospital. There, Dr. George Draper took over the case. He had been an associate of Lovett's and a colleague of Roosevelt's at Harvard.

When Roosevelt arrived at Presbyterian, he was still flat on his back. He had just enough strength in his arms to lift and turn himself. Dr. Draper arranged to have a strap hung over the bed so that Roosevelt could perform that function. But he still stayed on his back in bed most of the first days in the hospital. He resumed some business and political activity, dictating letters while staring straight at the ceiling. Dr. Lovett had warned Eleanor back at Campobello that adult victims of polio often displayed "mental depression" and "irritability." So far Roosevelt was putting up a good front, however, though the progress was not encouraging to his doctors. A week after Roosevelt entered Presbyterian, Dr. Draper wrote Dr. Lovett: "I am much concerned at the very slow recovery both as regards the disappearance of pain, which is generally present, and as to the recovery of even the slightest power to twitch the muscles. There is marked falling away of the muscle masses on either side of the spine in the lower lumbar region, likewise the buttocks. . . ." Roosevelt had entered the hospital believing he would soon be up and about on crutches. He wrote friends and even casual acquaintances to that effect.

Two weeks after he went into the hospital, he wrote Walter Camp a bittersweet letter. Camp was the football coach and writer who had conducted fitness classes for government officials in Washington during the war. Roosevelt told him that if he could get up out of bed and "join . . . in a sprint for the record, I would consider it the greatest joy in the world." He said his doctors led him to believe he would be vigorous again "sometime in the future."

It was not until several days after that that he sat up for the first time. With his strap arrangement and a nurse and doctor at his side, he was able in October to swing from bed to wheelchair. He could sit up in bed with back supports. On October 28, he was discharged from the hos-

22

pital and went to his home on 65th Street. He had not been discharged because he was cured, nor was his ordeal of pain over. In January 1922, the muscles behind his knees suddenly began to tighten, causing the legs to bend to grotesque posture. The treatment for this condition consisted of swathing the legs in plaster casts to arrest the movement, then using wedges to stretch the legs back to their normal position. It was not until the following month, after he was fitted with two leg braces, that Roosevelt found himself upright again. Then only with crutches and the braces could he stand and maneuver.

His progress continued at Hyde Park that summer. He had a trapeze device installed over his bed, which enabled him to exercise with leg raises. There was also a device that enabled him to swing from bed to wheelchair by himself, if the chair was held steady by someone else. His will to walk was transcendent. With crutches and braces, he decided to walk from the house to Route 9. That was the goal. The distance was only a quarter of a mile. Roosevelt typically set out accompanied by a relative, friend or servant pushing a wheelchair. Roosevelt chatted as he walked. The effort looked awkward, but the most significant aspect of it was its strenuousness. Usually, Roosevelt almost immediately broke out in a heavy sweat. He never made Route 9. His best effort that summer was just over halfway. Then his companion swung the wheelchair up, Roosevelt got in, and back they went to the house. (On occasions he took a walk on the grounds alone. Sometimes he fell or just ran out of energy. Then, he waited on the ground for help. According to one story, once he dragged himself to a tree and pulled himself upright.) The heavy sweating that accompanied his efforts to walk remained a characteristic.

Years later, when he had to walk in public—always with assistance—perspiration would pop out on his forehead and neck and stain his clothes.

The braces were cumbersome devices of leather and metal that covered his legs from ankle to hip. Each weighed seven pounds. They worked this way: The wearer, while seated, extended his legs straight out and donned the apparatus. A lock behind the knee joint was put in place so that no bending could occur. Then the wearer was lifted, or lifted himself, into an upright position. Upright and with crutches, Roosevelt could "walk." He was unsteady and tipped over at first. The crutches pained his armpits. This walking was really with his torso and arms, not his legs, whose muscles had still not come back. The exercising that Roosevelt had confidently predicted in December would allow him to progress to where he could walk without a limp by spring was not miraculous.

Another exercise Roosevelt began at Hyde Park was swinging from and walking alongside parallel bars. He had the bars set up on the south lawn and invited friends out to chat with him while he walked and walked and walked. Another leg exercise was to be pushed on a three-wheel cycle.

He also began to swim. Polio victims found warm water soothing physically and psychologically. Roosevelt ordered a pool built on the Hyde Park estate. Before it was ready, he used other pools in the area for his swimming therapy. He wrote Dr. Draper that he was taking a swim three times a week. "The legs work wonderfully in the water. . . . I see continuous improvement in my knees and feet." He added that he had become so strong in the arms that he could move from one chair to another just on sheer arm strength.

He said he often left his braces off when he had no need to stand or walk. By September, he could write Dr. Lovett that he could stand (in his braces) for an hour "without feeling tired" and without losing his balance. He said proudly that he could climb stairs with crutches and a handrail. His preferred method of going upstairs, however, was to sit down (without braces) and back up, using his arms to lift himself from stair to stair.

At the end of September in 1922, Roosevelt returned to 65th Street. The need to return to work was pressing. He needed the money, the activity and the opportunity to demonstrate that he was not an invalid. In the city, Roosevelt had two jobs and two offices. He was the New York representative of his friend Van Lear Black's Maryland Fidelity and Deposit Company, a bonding firm, with offices at 120 Broadway, and a partner in the law firm of Emmett, Marvin and Roosevelt, with offices at 52 Wall Street. The latter office building had a long flight of stairs. Partly because of that, Roosevelt returned to active business life only at 120 Broadway. Despite the lack of stairs there, a man in Roosevelt's condition had no easy time of it. He had to be assisted by his chauffeur across the sidewalk and the polished floor of the building's lobby. Basil O'Connor, who had an office in the building, first encountered Roosevelt in that lobby. Roosevelt had fallen, entering the building. A crowd gathered, and Roosevelt required both the chauffeur and a strong bystander to get him back on his feet.

More often, Roosevelt would have his chauffeur push him into the building in a wheelchair. He always did that when the weather was bad. When the weather was extremely bad, he did not go to the office at all.

Roosevelt was allowed to follow an individualized work

schedule at Fidelity and Deposit. His normal day involved coming in a little late in the morning, working straight through till 4:30—lunch at his desk—then home to exercise. He only worked every other week. Soon he was down to a four-day week. He retained his partnership in the law firm, but practiced little law from his desk at 120 Broadway. In 1924, he resigned from the firm, saying his health required him to spend two months each winter and some time in the summer out of the city.

The winters out of the city meant following the sun to Florida. The first winter back in New York after he learned to stand upright and move, he, Howe and John Lawrence, a Boston banker who'd been at Harvard with Roosevelt, rented a houseboat for a cruise to the Florida Keys. Eleanor and others joined them. Lawrence also had crippled legs. Roosevelt thought sun and salt water were very beneficial; he wrote Dr. Lovett that his calf muscles were increasing so in size that he would have to get his braces adjusted. When he returned to Hyde Park after the cruise, he noticed that his right leg had grown stronger than his left. He began some exercising with the right brace off.

The next winter, Roosevelt and Lawrence decided to buy their own houseboat. They renamed their new possession the *Larooco*—after Lawrence and Roosevelt; the seven letters and a double "o" were traditional sailors' bids for luck. Roosevelt spent the next three winters seeking balm and cure in the warm waters of south Florida. The gently sloping beaches and buoyant salt water made it easier for men with weakened legs to seek a depth and stand. Roosevelt described a routine day to his mother in a letter dated February 22, 1924. He and a companion had taken a motorboat ride to an inlet, "fished, got out on the sandy beach, picnicked and swam and lay in the sun for hours. I know it is doing the legs good, and though I have worn the braces hardly at all, I get lots of exercise crawling around, and I know the muscles are better than ever."

But Roosevelt was still looking for a cure. It had been over two years since he was stricken, and probably it was too late to find a cure. It may always have been. Experts in the treatment of the sort of polio lameness Roosevelt suffered agree that if muscle strength doesn't come back fairly soon, it doesn't come back at all. In 1923 and 1924, neither the patient nor the experts were that sure about this, however.

Roosevelt looked into everything. There was a doctor in Kansas City who recommended "aero-therapeutic" treatment. Some osteopaths had another approach: therapy with deep-heat lamps. Roosevelt looked abroad for cures, and not only conventional ones. A Wall Street friend wrote him that his wife was working with Dr. Emile Coue at Nancy. He was the advocate of positive thinking as a cure for ailments. Roosevelt urged the friend to relay his case history to Dr. Coue, whom he called "a really remarkable soul." That letter, dated September 4, 1924, told also of his intention to go to a new place he heard about to seek a cure, Warm Springs, Georgia, "where there is a huge outdoor pool of warm water which gushes from a hillside."

Roosevelt had returned to political prominence not long before he wrote that letter. From the first hours of his paralysis, he and, especially, Louis Howe had been concerned about the effect on his political future of stories to the effect that he was an invalid. While he was still flat on his back at Presbyterian, he had accepted membership on the Executive Committee of the Democratic Party of the

State of New York. He turned down suggestions that he seek office in 1922 and 1924, but he kept up a steady correspondence with Democratic leaders in New York and across the nation, suggesting ideas and strategies, and keeping his name before them. In 1924, confident at last after three years of recuperation, treatment and exercise—and practice—he agreed to appear in the spotlight. He would nominate Al Smith as the Democratic presidential candidate at Madison Square Garden.

He not only practiced walking in general; he practiced walking along the specific route he would follow in the Garden. The weeks before the nomination, he and his chauffeur, Louis Depew, walked back and forth in front of his Hyde Park home. He locked his braces, slipped his crutch under his right arm, grasped Depew's arm with his left hand and lurched forward with his shoulders, arms and torso providing the motive power. He also practiced sitting down in and getting up from the special chair Louis Howe had arranged for him on the convention floor. Unlike the others, it had arms. It was also prearranged that it would be positioned on the aisle. He chose his son James, 16 years old, to walk with him at Madison Square Garden. They practiced the walk there. James led him along, carrying his second crutch. When he got to the lectern, he grasped it with both hands and acknowledged the crowd's cheers with what he would make a gesture of appreciation and acknowledgment as recognizable as the politician's traditional wave of the arm: He threw his head back, thrust out his chin, and smiled broadly. When he finished speaking, and proving, or appearing to, that he was an able-bodied man, he allowed his wheelchair to be brought up to carry him away.

That was in June. On October 3, Roosevelt made his first

visit to the place he had heard had provided a cure for another polio victim, Warm Springs. He learned of the place at the convention from Charles Foster Peabody, a Wall Streeter whose home at Columbus, Georgia, was near Warm Springs. Roosevelt spent three weeks there, liked it, returned the following spring for six weeks. He thought it offered the elusive cure he still believed in, but he also kept investigating other avenues to health. In August of 1925, after two visits to Georgia, he went to Marion, Massachusetts, to work with Dr. William McDonald. Roosevelt's uncle, Fred Delano, sent him there. Louis Howe had a vacation cottage nearby. FDR took his chauffeur and another manservant with him, to assist him back and forth from a rented cottage to the doctor's place. McDonald encouraged Roosevelt's natural optimism by promising to get him on his feet without braces. Roosevelt began swimming and exercising on a walking board. Because the water was not as warm as at the Georgia spa, he soon found he couldn't stay in as long. Three other patients, all teen-agers, stayed there, too. By December, Roosevelt walked a block with a cane and a single brace. He thought he was on the way to unaided walking, but his progress to the cane and brace was the high point of that cure. The next summer he returned but noticed no improvement.

By then he had already committed himself to buying Warm Springs and turning what was then only a somewhat run-down resort into a combination health and vacation facility. The previous winter he had taken his last cruise on the *Larooco*.

Agents of Peabody came down to discuss with him the purchase of the Georgia property in February and again in March on the *Larooco*. Roosevelt signed the papers in

Warm Springs in April. "I seemed to have bought Warm Springs," he wrote his mother.

## A note on sources for this chapter

In addition to the general sources mentioned before, I drew principally on the book *A Good Fight* by Jean Gould. The best description of the onset of FDR's polio is found in the series of letters dealing with the period in *FDR: His Personal Letters,* edited by Elliott Roosevelt. The best description of the 1924 nomination is in James Roosevelt's book, *My Parents: A Differing View.*

# On the Map

---

Creek Indians discovered healing properties in the warm mineral waters that gushed from the side of Pine Mountain in southwest Georgia. Their white supplanters found the waters and the mountain more suited to relaxation than therapy. For nearly 100 years before Franklin Roosevelt made his first visit to Warm Springs, the community had been a summer vacation resort. Its elevation (over 1,200 feet) and the thick pine forests that gave the mountain its name made for pleasant temperatures even in the dog days of the deepest South. A town grew up around the resort and was incorporated as Bullochville in 1896 (named after Eleanor Roosevelt's father's mother's family). The hotel that Roosevelt would see (but never stay in) was the Meriwether Inn, built in 1889 to replace a hotel which had burned down. It was a three-story rambling green, yellow and white Victorian monstrosity, with eccentric turrets and verandas. It had two tiny enclosed pools for men and women and an outdoor pool 150 feet by 50 feet, large by the standards of the day. But by the end of World War I, the resort had fallen on hard times. The owner, Charles Lamar Davis, seemed to have lost his grip on the enterprise. A newspaper editor from Columbus, Thomas W. Loyless, remembered the hotel at the turn of the century, and thought its grandeur could be restored. He leased the property from Davis, with an option to buy, in 1919 or 1920. He paid Davis $9,000 a year, and lost money each year. He was seldom able to fill the 46-room hotel and its 15 small cabins for the summer season. In a 1937 talk to patients at Warm Springs, Roosevelt put it this way: "The old place had fallen on rather thin days and when I came down here in the fall of 1924, they had a very poor season, and the man who ran the hotel—well, he was in the red and most of his knives and forks had disappeared and most of the crockery had been broken." What had been a famous place was now down at the heels.

In 1923 Loyless met George Foster Peabody in New York. Peabody was from Columbus, Georgia. Loyless had gone to New York to augment his summer income from the hotel. He told Peabody about his efforts and about a young man who claimed to have been "cured" of polio by swimming in the waters at Warm Pine Mountain. Peabody expressed interest in joining Loyless in the enterprise. He had Loyless ask the young man, Louis Joseph, to write a letter for Roosevelt, describing his experiences. Peabody conveyed the letter to Roosevelt, invited him down to the resort. He gave Loyless money to paint the inn and spruce up the grounds a little.

Roosevelt, Eleanor, Marguerite (Missy) LeHand, his personal secretary, and Irwin McDuffie, his valet, took a train down from New York, arriving at Bullochville's small station on October 3. The "season" was over, but a small staff remained at the hotel, including Louis Joseph. The pool was still open. When the train arrived at dusk, Tom Loyless was there to greet Roosevelt. So was Miss Georgia Wilkins, Davis's niece. They had a direct interest in the visitor. Roosevelt's fame as a leading Democratic light attracted also the mayor, E. B. Doyle, a farmer; the town's one physician, Dr. Neal Kitchens; the Columbus couple whose cottage Roosevelt would stay in, the Harts; and a number of others, over 50 in all. Most were just curious.

Roosevelt was lifted down from the Pullman platform by McDuffie and a young black man Loyless had brought with him. The celebrity's braces had been locked so that he could walk to the platform from inside the Pullman car. Once aground, he walked on crutches again to a waiting car. One observer, Ruth Stevens, later recorded her impression of a robust man with legs "like spaghetti." His wheelchair was loaded in with the other baggage, and off the party went to the Hart cottage, murmuring proper appreciative remarks about the clean air and handsome pines, ignoring the signs of rural southern poverty in the town and on the clay road to the resort area, several hundred yards away.

The Roosevelts settled in at the Hart cottage. Years later, reminiscing about that first night, FDR said he was kept awake by the sounds of squirrels running across the roof. The next morning, he waited at the cottage for Louis Joseph. Joseph was a 26-year-old engineer who had been stricken in much the same fashion Roosevelt had in 1920. He had been paralyzed from the waist down. When he had recovered enough to travel, he left his New York home for his father's cottage on Pine Mountain in 1921. He stayed two years there and in Columbus. He spent a lot of time swimming in the warm waters. He could not walk when he first came down, but he seemed to have swum his way back to health. He worked at the inn in the summer of 1924 as a clerk. He stayed at the request of Loyless and Peabody to talk to Roosevelt after the hotel closed.

Roosevelt questioned him closely about his lameness, his progress, his exercises, and how much he attributed his success to Warm Springs. Joseph's success was in the nature of what Roosevelt had always hoped for himself. He could walk without assistance, and often did at home, but he usually employed one cane.

After a chat with Joseph, Loyless drove Roosevelt and his valet to the pool. They arranged a private dressing room with drapes of canvas in the bathhouse. Roosevelt may have swum with Joseph that morning—he did, either that day or the next, and discussed the water's effects with Joseph's doctor, Dr. James Johnson of the nearby textile town of Manchester. FDR's first dip, solo or accompanied, was on October 4 and brought the exclamation that he had never felt any water so pleasant. He said he was able to lift his right leg, the stronger one. Joseph told Roosevelt that he had progressed from standing and walking in neck- or chest-deep water till he could stand and walk in shallower and shallower water. Finally, he could walk without the water's support. Roosevelt picked that up as a means of measuring his progress at Warm Springs. Later, he would write friends that he could stand and walk in so many fewer inches depth, which he would translate as meaning his legs had strengthened to the point of being able to carry so many more pounds. He was quite specific about it, but probably not quite scientific.

Roosevelt could very soon stand and walk with ease in
four feet of water. Perhaps he could have done that in any
water. But the Warm Springs water did have different mineral qualities—double molecules of magnesium and cal-
cium—that gave it a higher specific gravity than most spring
water. It was, according to the therapists who came there to
work in the following years, the most buoyant freshwater
they had ever encountered.

Eleanor Roosevelt went back to New York shortly after
her husband was settled in the Hart cottage. Missy stayed
to help him with some work. He was writing politicians
around the country, and doing some work for Fidelity and
Deposit. Basil O'Connor, whom Roosevelt had gotten to
know at 120 Broadway and with whom he was negotiating
about forming a new law partnership, apparently came
down to conclude that discussion. Otherwise, Roosevelt devoted his time to swimming and working out in the pool
twice a day, for an hour or more. Other times, he'd relax at
cards, chat with the few people who remained at the hotel
or in cabins, and with the town's gossipy mailman. Sometimes, he'd ride about the countryside. Loyless drove him
in a car which some county business and political leaders
provided. He attended at least one large cocktail party at
the resort and went to a civic club meeting in Manchester.
He also attended a ceremony at which the town's name of
Bullochville was officially changed to Warm Springs. Perhaps with a joking reference to that, Loyless later told
Roosevelt that he "certainly put Warm Springs on the
map." But what he really had reference to was something
that did more than a name change to make Warm Springs
well known.

Almost two weeks after Roosevelt arrived in Georgia, a

reporter for the *Atlanta Journal* took the two-hour trip down from Atlanta. His name was Cleburne Gregory. His editor, Jack Cohen, was an active Democrat. He knew of Roosevelt and may have talked with him about Warm Springs at the New York convention. At any rate, Gregory interviewed Roosevelt, observed his workouts, then wrote a Sunday supplement for his paper for the edition of October 26, the day Roosevelt left Warm Springs. Because of the effect of the article and because it is such a good first-hand account, it is worth quoting at length.

"Franklin D. Roosevelt, New York lawyer and banker, Assistant Secretary of the Navy during the World War, and Democratic nominee for Vice President in 1920, is literally swimming his way back to health and strength at Warm Springs, Georgia. . . ."

After reviewing Roosevelt's medical history, Gregory continued: "Mr. Roosevelt and Mr. Loyless, in adjoining cottages, are the only residents of the dozen or more small cottages surrounding the Warm Springs hotel at the present time. The hotel has closed for the winter season. . . . The distinguished visitor has the large swimming pool to himself two hours or more each day. . . .

"He swims, dives, uses the swinging rings and horizontal bar over the water and finally crawls out on the concrete pier for a sun bath that lasts another hour. Then he dresses, has lunch, rests a bit on the delightfully shady porch, and spends the afternoon driving over the countryside, in which he is intensely interested. . . .

" 'I am deriving wonderful benefit from my stay here,' Mr. Roosevelt said. 'This place is great. See that right leg? It is the first time I have been able to move it at all in three years.' Mr. Roosevelt does not attribute any medicinal effects to the Warm Springs water, but he gives the water credit for his ability to remain in it for two hours or more, without tiring in the least, and the rest of the credit for his improvement is given to Georgia's sunshine.

" 'The best infantile paralysis expert in New York told me that the only way to overcome the effects of the disease was to swim as much as possible and bask in the sunlight. Conditions here are ideal for both prescriptions. The water in some way relaxes muscles drawn taut by the disease and gives the limbs much greater action. The sunshine has curative effects, I understand.'

"So marked have the benefits been in his case, Mr. Roosevelt plans to return to Warm Springs in March or April and remain two or three months. At that time he will build a cottage on the hilltop. . . ."

As if that description were not enough to attract polio sufferers everywhere to Warm Springs—how that sentence about moving his right leg for the first time in three years must have leapt from the page!—Gregory concluded by saying that George Foster Peabody, his nephew Charles Peabody, and Tom Loyless planned to spend "millions" to create a "year-round health resort" there.

The article appeared not only in the *Journal* but in papers everywhere after the *Journal* syndicated it. In some newspapers, the curative aspects of swimming were accentuated, or rather exaggerated, by linking the Roosevelt article with "bathing beauties" elsewhere, including Annette Kellerman, a famous swimmer, who had supposedly been cured of polio's aftereffects by swimming. Immediately the mail began to pour into the Warm Springs post office from polios and their families asking about facilities for the coming summer.

And not only mail. When Roosevelt came back to Warm Springs on April 1, 1925, after a winter cruise aboard the *Larooco*, it was to a town that was beginning to attract hopeful cripples from all over the country.

One was Fred Botts, a cadaverous young man from Elizabethville, Pennsylvania, who would remain in Warm Springs as registrar of the Georgia Warm Springs Foundation. His role in the business affairs of the foundation, plus his active participation in the social life of the foundation at Thanksgiving and on other presidential visits—and year round—were enough to make him a legend, but Roosevelt assured him celebrity by repeating at public events a slightly exaggerated story about Botts's arrival at Warm Springs the day after Roosevelt himself arrived in 1925. According to Roosevelt, Botts was so thin and bony he sank. But Roosevelt taught him how to begin the swim back to health. Botts's own memories of that first April in Georgia were only slightly different.

He came down with his brother and his wheelchair on the train the same day Roosevelt came up from Florida. His brother carried him to the hotel, where he was assigned a room in one of the cottages. It was "immaculate," he noticed, but the walls were whitewashed instead of plastered, the screens were all badly torn, there were cracks in the roof. He and a few other early arrivals (the "season" didn't open till May 1) listened to Tom Loyless outline his hopes for the resort. The next day his brother took him to the pool. He was wheeled from car to poolside. Several people were already at play in the pool. Two weren't playing. They were polios—Mrs. Thelma Steiger of Jefferson City, Missouri, and Lambert Hirsheimer of Falmouth Heights, Massachusetts. Before Roosevelt arrived at about

11 A.M., other cure-seekers joined them in the water to swim, or—in Botts's case—to paddle supported by inner tubes. Paul Rogers, a well-to-do businessman from Milwaukee who was also to become a regular, and a young Boston victim, Elizabeth Retan, were there that day.

Even more famous than Botts in Warm Springs lore is a woman Roosevelt always identified as "a lady from St. Louis who weighed about two hundred pounds." Apparently her name was Miss Dorothy Weaver. She and a companion or relative came to the pool that first day shortly after Roosevelt arrived. Roosevelt recalled the day in public speeches several times in future visits to Warm Springs. He usually linked her "case" with Botts's. In a speech at Warm Springs in March 1937, he put it like this: "Old Dr. Roosevelt finally persuaded Fred to see if he could put his legs down to the bottom of the pool. That was easy, because they did not have any flesh on them anyway. But when it came to the lady, that was different. Old Dr. Roosevelt put the lady alongside the edge of the pool—there was a handrail there —and I said, 'Just concentrate. Use your mind. Just think about getting that leg down to the bottom of the pool.' Well, she would get about halfway down and then I would take hold of her right leg and push a little and push a little and finally got the whole leg down to the bottom of the pool. And finally I said, 'Concentrate and hold it there.' And she would say, 'I have it there!' And then, gently, I would move over to get the left leg down and as I moved the left leg down, up came the right leg.' ".

This story never failed to get a laugh from the polios at Warm Springs. That night they drowned out his next line: "So you see, these girls who think they are physiotherapists don't know anything about it. I invented it first."

There is far more than a grain of truth in that. He *was* a pioneer therapist. That first summer, he and Dr. James Johnson of nearby Manchester were the sole sources of professional advice available to the influx of cripples. Johnson was a small-town doctor with no specialized training in orthopedics. Roosevelt said he called on Johnson to make sure that none of the patients had any other health problems that would make exercise in the pool undesirable. Later, the two worked out charts for measuring muscle growth and strength. Roosevelt overstated or overappraised his own technical knowledge, according to some who have studied his life. Undoubtedly, on occasion, he did. He had a way of exaggerating when he was in an anecdotal mood. But he did know a lot about wasting diseases and, especially, about therapy in 1925. He had spent four years studying. As he wrote Dr. George Draper in New York later that year from Dr. McDonald's place at Marion, Massachusetts, ". . . I have seen the methods of practically all the other doctors in the country—the Lovett method, Goldthwaite method, Hibbs method, St. Louis method, Chicago method, etc., etc. . . ." Then he discussed in a technically knowledgeable way the principles McDonald's and the various other methods were based on.

There was an even dozen polios at Warm Springs that first summer, not counting Dr. Roosevelt. They stayed at a private home, in a boarding house in town, and at the whitewashed little cottages circling the inn, one of which, large enough for several guests, was in such disrepair that Roosevelt dubbed it "the Wreck." And some stayed at the rambling old yellow and green Meriwether Inn itself. It opened that year under a new corporation headed by Loyless, and for the first time it invited "invalids" as well as

other seekers of relaxation and pleasure. Roosevelt undoubtedly began thinking about taking an even more active
role in the resort's development than those of "doctor" and,
as he also described himself half in jest during this period,
"consulting engineer and landscape architect." Loyless
sought Roosevelt's advice on a variety of matters. Loyless
was also clearly ailing (he had cancer, Roosevelt learned at
Marion, in a letter from Loyless's sister). Roosevelt had to
be aware that he could not manage the ambitious under-
taking alone for long. When he came back to Georgia in
the spring of 1926 for a five-week visit, again from a Florida
cruise on the *Larooco*, he probably came ready to buy it
and take it over.

There were two explanations for that. One, Roosevelt
was an adventurous businessman. He had been involved
in a number of imaginative—even reckless—schemes over
the years. He had put money in a plan to fly passenger diri-
gibles from New York to Chicago. He had tried to corner
the lobster market. He had invested in wildcat oil wells. A
second reason Warm Springs attracted him was that it had
an undeveloped look. Eleanor Roosevelt liked to recall,
years later, that he was always restless to improve run-down
or desolate landscapes. He told her once he would like to
go to some desert land in the Middle East after the war and
create a garden there. (He urged Arab officials at a meeting
during the war to explore for water under their sands.) He
may even have expected to turn a profit on Warm Springs;
Florida's land boom was in full flower at the time. And
there may have been a third reason. As costly as Warm
Springs could become, he was already spending a fortune
on his health. Counting his Georgia, Florida and Massachusetts trips, the cost of the pool at Hyde Park, and the

expenses of the *Larooco*, Roosevelt spent over $14,000 in his health search in 1925 and approximately $10,000 in 1926.

Peabody offered the property to Roosevelt for $200,000. Loyless had died while FDR was cruising off Florida that winter. At the end of 1923, he had, with Peabody's financial backing, exercised the option to buy the property for $100,000. As of the spring of 1926, $60,000 of that was still owed to Charles Davis's heir, Miss Georgia Wilkins, by a Peabody Corporation that had acquired full rights. Some, if not all, of the $40,000 Miss Wilkins had received, Peabody had paid. He had also spent some money on operating the property in 1924 and 1925, presumably, and had to pay off the $60,000 balance. Still, he made a nice deal out of it. Roosevelt, with his new law partner Basil O'Connor unenthusiastically handling some of the details, agreed to pay $195,000 for the property once it was unencumbered. The terms were as follows: $25,000 cash, $50,000 to Miss Wilkins by the end of 1928, $10,000 a year to Peabody for ten years, with a final payment of $20,000 at the end of that time. Possession was to be immediate, but deeds weren't to be delivered until February 1927.

That was a substantial debt for Roosevelt to accept. He was well-to-do, but no millionaire. Not counting property he had begun to buy around the hotel property, including cottages, lots and farm property, Roosevelt's assets at the end of 1926 were about $275,000—$187,406.50 in stocks, $63,228 in bonds, $23,337.86 in cash. His investments in Georgia totaled just over $100,000 as of that time—and the prospects of that producing income were remote. Thus, he had, in a sense, taken on an obligation in Georgia that many would consider out of proportion to his wealth. It has often been said he was risking two-thirds of his fortune, but the intricacies of the laws regarding corporate liabilities are such that this probably is an overstatement. Still, his debt of approximately $200,000 and his desire to keep the endeavor going meant that for the foreseeable future he would carry a heavy financial burden for a man whose earned and unearned income was between $60,000 and $80,000 a year at a time.

## *A note on sources for this chapter*

Turnley Walker's *Roosevelt and the Warm Springs Story* is indispensable in writing about Roosevelt's life in Georgia. The information on Roosevelt's financial situation comes from his annual statements, which are at the Roosevelt Library at Hyde Park. Fred Botts wrote a reminiscence of his first days at Warm Springs, which is now at the Library. Rex Tugwell interviewed Louis Joseph and a number of other people who knew Roosevelt in Warm Springs. Some of the interviews, which were tape-recorded, have been transcribed; some are still just available for listening. The transcripts and the tapes are at Hyde Park.

# The Key Man

What Roosevelt had actually bought was a somewhat run-down summer hotel without steam heat, but with naturally warm mineral-water swimming pools, over 1,000 acres of woodland on the side of a mountain, a handful of dilapidated whitewashed cottages, a few cottages of better construction, and a dream of combining two unlikely functions —therapy for crippled individuals and relaxation for well-to-do vacationers. On April 27, 1926, just eight days after the deed transferring the property to Roosevelt's new organization was signed, an Associated Press story appeared in the *New York Times*, announcing the new setup and saying, "Mr. Roosevelt said he expects to make the property an all-year resort." The *Times* followed this up, presumably with a telephone call, and on the 28th a story under a *Times* credit line said Roosevelt "and several associates are now the owners of the resort. Mr. Roosevelt believes that the Springs can be made a national resort, and plans to that end are being made. It is believed that he will interest many

44

prominent Easterners and that the Springs soon will rank with the most frequented resorts in the country."

Easterners *and* southerners were in Roosevelt's sight, and part of the operation would be not just a resort but a club. He explained that selected individuals from North and South could enjoy the benefits of Warm Springs by sharing privately built and owned cottages. In his words: "The cottage owners from the North would be glad to turn their cottages over to the members from the South in the summer, and Southerners would be glad to turn their cottages over to the Northern members in the winter, as the club membership qualifications would assure a personnel which would take care of all the properties and maintain them properly."

It was Roosevelt, not the newspapers, who was putting the emphasis on the high-class social-resort half of the project. In a press release issued at this time, he spoke of development that would "first" get the "famous Warm Springs baths and swimming pools" back into operation. "Second will be the erection, possibly this fall, of a health resort which will accommodate patients suffering from infantile paralysis and kindred afflictions, which have been relieved by the waters there." To those brief matter-of-fact statements was added this: "Third, the building of a cottage colony around the magnificent country club as a community center which will be available to people who are willing to maintain their part of the colony on a scale in keeping with their resources and their positions in life." And on and on about plans for an eighteen-hole golf course, bridle paths, shooting preserves, a fishing lake, a "magnificent" clubhouse.

Roosevelt did envision a first-class resort for first-class

people, somewhat in the style of what he imagined the place to have been in its early days before the Civil War. Years later, when that dream had proved empty, replaced by the greater dream of an internationally known treatment center for polio patients, Roosevelt liked to remind the patients there, many of them from middle- and lower-income backgrounds, that Warm Springs a century before had been "a famous place," where the likes of Henry Clay and John C. Calhoun had cavorted. Roosevelt kept emphasizing this aspect that year—perhaps because of his romantic attachment to that past, or perhaps because of two friendships he was developing in Warm Springs: with the wealthy, very social industrialists Henry Pope of Chicago and James T. Whitehead of Detroit, each of whom had a daughter with polio. Or perhaps because he believed the economics of the thing demanded a successful nontherapeutic side to the project. His explanation that fall to an Atlanta *Georgian* reporter led to another newspaper story. It read: "The new Meriwether Reserve [the official title given the corporation that ran both the polio and the nonpolio-related commercial activities] will rival Pinehurst in the North Carolina Mountains." The amenities would include, Roosevelt now said, *two* eighteen-hole golf courses.

In fact, there would eventually be only one nine-hole golf course, and Roosevelt probably knew or had begun to suspect even in the fall of 1926 that his Warm Springs would be a different sort of spa than the Pinehursts of the world. That first season opened in May of 1926 amid contradictory omens. Here is how an observer who was there described the hotel in May: "It looked like an old-time hostelry in any quiet mountain resort of the Eastern states. Porch chairs, a great dining room, with Negro waiters, parked automobiles with state licenses from far and near, big trees of oak and pine, and under them a midget golf course. Only after a first look did you see the fleet of wheel-chairs, filled for the most part with youth, and the crutches, canes and braces. But nothing there seemed like a hospital or sanatarium. It had the spirit of a country club."

There were about twice as many "able-bodied" vaca-tioners that year as polios, and each group complained to the management about the other. The vacationers were worried about becoming infected by sharing a pool with the polios, and the polios resented the disapproving looks they got. Separate exercise pools had been dug near the larger pool, and a dining room was set up in the basement of the hotel for the exclusive use of the polios, but in-teraction was impossible to avoid. Roosevelt desperately wanted the income from the vacationers, but he certainly did not go to great lengths to create separate colonies. His nine-hole golf course was designed to his specification that polio victims who could play but not walk, or who could neither play nor walk but wanted to watch others play, would be able to drive along the course from tee to hole to tee. That meant, among other things, wider, strong bridges over the few streams on the course so that autos could drive across.

Some of Roosevelt's friends and some of the growing staff at Warm Springs suggested to him that he concentrate on the therapeutic half of the operation, even to the point of abandoning efforts to build a Georgia "Pinehurst." Louis Howe wrote him on April 1, 1927, with advice in April Fool-ish fashion: "As every patent medicine faker has dis-covered, nothing does the 'come on' like a before and after photograph. Why, God only knows. . . . Perhaps just one photograph showing them doing a hundred-yard dash or shoveling coal or something or another after treatment, together with the statement that, when they arrived, it required two stretchers and an ambulance to get them down to the pool, might do the trick."

It wasn't funny. Even had Roosevelt felt he didn't need the money from the nonpolios, there was a problem involved in making Warm Springs into a recognized health facility, one that need not depend on publicity for patients, but would get referrals from physicians. Roosevelt had hired a medical staff in 1926. Dr. Leroy W. Hubbard, who had just retired from the New York State Board of Health, came down as surgeon in chief. He was preceded by his chief aide, Helena Mahoney, who had the title of Director of Nurses. Both had had experience with polio patients, but she had a more dynamic personality than he; for the first few years she probably had more to do with the development of the after-care programs than did Dr. Hubbard or "Dr." Roosevelt. Dr. Hubbard had 13 years' experience as an orthopedic surgeon dealing with after-care of polio patients; that was important.

Warm Springs had difficulty getting the professional acceptance that Roosevelt wanted at the start. The American Orthopedic Association held its annual meeting in Atlanta the spring Roosevelt bought Warm Springs. He went to Atlanta and lobbied with orthopedists and association officials to get Warm Springs in some way supported by the association. They turned him down. Undoubtedly, that was in part due to the fact that Dr. Johnson, who was then the resident expert, was not an orthopedic surgeon or a full-time employee of the spa.

Despite that setback, and because of the friction between

polios and vacationers, Roosevelt decided in 1927 to make
Warm Springs a health spa, not a resort. The corporation
that had been established with profit-making as a goal was
replaced by the Georgia Warm Springs Foundation, Inc.
Roosevelt was president, as he had been of the initial corporation. The trustees of the foundation were all directors
of the earlier corporation: Dr. Hubbard, George Foster Peabody, and the two businessmen whose daughters' polio had
introduced them to Warm Springs and Roosevelt, Henry
Pope and James Whitehead. It was obviously Roosevelt's
belief that wealthy individuals like Peabody, Pope and
Whitehead would support the venture as a favorite philanthropy. But in the next few years, he was the principal,
though not exclusive, supporter of his dream. It was his
money, or the guarantee of it, that made it possible for the
gap between inadequate income and the costs of the enterprise to be made up.

The early effort of the venture proved costly. Dr. Hubbard and Mahoney were joined by a physiotherapist, Helen
Lauer, then another and soon a corps of "physios," as they
were called. These were young female graduates in physical
education from Nashville's Peabody College. Their job was
to work with the patients in the pool, forcing them to move
muscles they couldn't move themselves, teaching them to
move muscles they only thought they couldn't move, developing strengths to compensate for muscles that would never
regain function. This was the central activity at Warm
Springs in the first years, before there was a hospital for
corrective surgery. The polios and the physios would get
into the pools together. The polio would sit, lie or be
strapped in some fashion, depending on the type of affliction, to an underwater table, and the physio would begin

49

coercing limb movement. There were also "obstacle courses" near the pool where the patients practiced walking in controlled simulation of the pedestrian's real world.

There were some dozen physios by 1928. Fred Botts had become registrar. Another polio, Arthur Carpenter, who came down from Connecticut for treatment in 1927, was soon to become business manager. There had been only 33 polios—or "companions" as they began to call themselves —at Warm Springs at the end of the 1926 season, by an unofficial count. In 1927, there were some 80 companions at an informal Thanksgiving dinner to end the season. Patients then were paying $42 a week for "room, board, treatment, use of the pool and transportation to and from the same," as Mahoney put it in a letter to Carpenter when he first inquired. Transportation from the inn or a cottage to the pool was necessary, since the yard distance was too far for almost all the polios, even the ones who could walk. It was provided first in an old touring car, then in a bus as the numbers increased. Able-bodied friends or relatives who accompanied those with afflictions paid $28 a week for room and board. Neither figure covered the true costs of the operation at that time.

Roosevelt was writing checks or signing notes with abandon. For example, in April 1927 he wrote checks to E. T. Curtis, then managing Meriwether Reserve, for $4,500 $5,000, $2,500, $2,000 and $6,800. That year all other contributions from friends totaled $12,000. "I knew that he was running this place, that he was backing everything up," Mary Veeder (née Hudson), who was a physiotherapist beginning in 1928, said years later. "The bills all went to Hyde Park." Roosevelt never gave up trying to entice others to contribute. In 1928, for example, when he learned that his Dutchess County friend, Henry Morganthau, had purchased and sold for him some stock at a $3,000 profit, Roosevelt wrote him that since he had forgotten to give him a check to buy the stock, why didn't they just split the profits—and both give $1,500 to Warm Springs' patient aid fund, a Roosevelt idea for helping those companions who did not come from the affluent strata of society that so many of the earlier ones represented.

There were some outside benefactors. Henry Pope, for one, was generous. So was Edsel Ford. He came down to visit his friend and fellow Detroiter, James Whitehead. He was impressed with what was going on and agreed to pay the full cost of a much-needed indoor pool. Roosevelt believed a year-round facility was needed. He was having steam heat installed in the inn. A covered pool would make a 12-month year possible (though few individual polios did stay for that long at a stretch). Despite these outside contributions, there was no doubt that Roosevelt was the "key man." His gifts to the foundation in that period could not be calculated with exactness, but were great. He was also lending the foundation money.

It was not just money he was providing. He was still "Dr." Roosevelt, suggesting therapies to patients and staff alike. He was also involved in such things as sketching a design for the Edsel Ford pool, designing a wheelchair that made it easier for him to move in and out of it, working out a new leg brace for patient Antoinette Bachelder when her old one became uncomfortable. And so on.

When in 1928 New York Democrats began to pressure him to run for governor, he fled to Warm Springs and begged off, claiming correctly, if conveniently, that his responsibilities there were too great. Al Smith and Eleanor

Roosevelt tracked him down by telephone, first in a drug-store, where he was lowered backward into a booth, his braced legs left straight out in the aisle, then in a second conversation back at the inn. Eight years later, Roosevelt wrote a memo for use by his staff in rebutting rumors that he was paid to run for governor by John J. Raskob, the General Motors executive. Raskob was campaign manager for the Democratic presidential nominee, Al Smith. He believed that a Roosevelt candidacy in New York would help Smith. Raskob got on the phone after Roosevelt got back to the inn and, according to Roosevelt's own later suggestion of an official account, here is what happened:

"The simple fact was that in 1928, during the New York State Convention, he was begged to run for Governor and replied that he did not wish to do so, first, because he was making such excellent progress in taking Infantile Paralysis treatments at Warm Springs, and secondly, he was engaged in trying to build up the Foundation and to extend its use-fulness. In this connection he told Mr. Raskob on the tele-phone that in this work he was trying to raise as much money as possible toward this end. Mr. Raskob replied that he and his friends would help in raising this money for the construction of much needed buildings at Warm Springs. Mr. Raskob volunteered that he personally would contrib-ute $50,000 to the Foundation. Since that date—October 1, 1928—he has contributed various sums but it is under-stood that the amount of $50,000 has never been made good...."

Roosevelt's memo was inaccurate about how much Ras-kob had contributed to Warm Springs; the eventual total was apparently over twice that promised. But he correctly perceived in 1928 that once he went back into elective politics and achieved governing responsibilities, his health and his project would have to be given somewhat less time than otherwise. The change in neither case was abrupt. His efforts to raise money for the foundation continued after his election in 1928. In a way, his being governor (he won a hair's-breadth victory, while Smith lost) gave him the sort of access to moneyed interests he might not have otherwise enjoyed, and he took advantage of that. On June 4, 1929, a few months after he took office as governor, he returned to New York City from a spring vacation in Warm Springs to address the Bankers Club about his pet project. William H. Woodin, a prominent Republican who served on the board of the foundation and later became Roosevelt's first Secretary of the Treasury, arranged the meeting.

Roosevelt spoke first as governor, describing the state's efforts in behalf of cripples. He painted a bleak picture. "There are somewhere around fifty thousand cripples in our state of New York . . . between forty thousand and fifty thousand have never received adequate medical treatment." He said that he wasn't being critical, nor did he have plans for the state under his leadership to do a great deal new about that. "It isn't a government function. As I have said before, the government, no state government, no national government, can afford to embark on a program that would look after the needs of 350,000 crippled persons in this country. It has got to be a development of private charity." However, he said that the state would undertake a more thorough census of crippled people than had ever been done before, and would also look into development of spas in the state. Then he went on to describe in enthusiastic terms the work at Warm Springs. He made it clear that was where his own dreams lay. He urged the bankers to come down for a look and told them how money spent there could benefit not only the patients there but cripples everywhere, as new understanding of the cause of the disease and after-care and rehabilitation came about.

Outside contributions did come in, but Roosevelt still had to subsidize his dream. In 1931, Haskins and Sells did an audit and concluded that "Meriwether Reserve, Inc., was indebted to you . . . in the amount of $115,633.11 on its note payable, plus accrued interest of $14,914.51." One reason that the burden fell on Roosevelt was that he was regarded as *too* "key." There is no doubt that many of the bankers in that June audience asked themselves and each other what would happen to Warm Springs if Roosevelt became unavailable, for one reason or another. The following year Roosevelt and Keith Morgan, an insurance man who had become the foundation's chief fund raiser, discussed the problem. Morgan believed that the foundation should be insured against Roosevelt's death—if not against his distraction by official responsibilities. He meant that literally. In the summer of 1930, as Roosevelt prepared for the campaign that would see him reelected, Morgan made this pitch in a letter to Basil O'Connor: "Many people have said to me, 'Well, what would be the status of Warm Springs if anything happened to Mr. Roosevelt? Would it be able to go on?' " He proposed that a life insurance policy with the foundation as beneficiary would signal potential contributors that Warm Springs "has set about making itself a permanent institution." O'Connor sent the letter to Roosevelt, who wrote back in September, "Dear Doc:—I can see no objection to the Foundation insuring my life if it wants to."

Morgan put together a group of 13 insurance companies who together insured Roosevelt for $560,000. The cost to the foundation was $24,676.55 the first year, less each year thereafter. Thenceforth, the financial burden that Roosevelt had accepted was lifted off his shoulders. The foundation did not immediately cast off its financial problems, but it did begin to find steadier financial footing. It would take a President Roosevelt to make the foundation the success— and then some—that Roosevelt, O'Connor, Morgan, Hubbard, Mahoney, Carpenter, Boggs and the rest of the early dreamers had hoped for.

In agreeing to run for governor of New York did Roosevelt sacrifice an opportunity to regain his health? To overcome his lameness? Many people believe so. Raskob himself wrote Roosevelt in December 1928 that "I never knew a man to make a greater sacrifice than you did in coming to the aid of our party." Elliott Roosevelt also thought his father forsook an opportunity to regain his ability to walk. Dr. Hubbard was quoted years later to the effect that he and Helena Mahoney counseled Roosevelt not to reenter politics. He reportedly said that Roosevelt could possibly regain 15 to 20 percent more strength in his legs and walk safely without braces.

After all, unrestricted access to therapy at Warm Springs had brought about obvious results: obvious to Roosevelt and to the public. In 1924 or shortly thereafter, Roosevelt had decided to improve on his comeback walk to the podium to nominate Al Smith at Madison Square Garden. For two years before the 1928 convention, which was held in Houston, Roosevelt practiced toward that specific goal in his new cottage at Warm Springs. At night after a day of rest and therapy and play, he and Mahoney worked on his balance. Back and forth across the floor of his living room he would walk on Mahoney's arm, using a single cane in his other hand (legs braced, of course). Elliott came down to practice the arm-and-cane walk. FDR emphasized to them both how important he felt it was for him to appear relaxed. Often he would say that with beads of sweat on his forehead, the result of the physical effort. On occasion, he practiced standing alone. He would walk to a wall using one crutch. He would stand with his back against the wall and push the crutch away. The first time he tried that, he fell. Eventually, he succeeded.

It all paid off. In Houston, the summer of 1928, he walked to the podium on Elliott's arm. He spread his legs wide, grasped the lectern with both hands, smiled that jut-jawed smile, as he had four years earlier in New York, then took one hand off the lectern and waved to the cheering delegates. He could walk without an arm, if he chose to, using two canes and two braces only. He believed he could eventually discard one of each.

His muscle tests in 1928 reportedly showed somewhat greater strength than when he first began testing them at Warm Springs. But that was probably minuscule improvement (the records are gone) and, in fact, many physicians and therapists who specialize in lower trunk and limb polio paralysis, including some who worked with Roosevelt, agree that further progress of the sort Roosevelt talked about was not probable. "He had below 50 percent use of muscles in his lower extremities," according to Alice Plastridge. "After five years, you can't expect to get improvement." Even had he done what he said he wanted to do the next four years, which was go to Warm Springs every few months, now that a cold-weather pool was there, he still would have had below 50 percent use, she reported. Roosevelt's real accomplishment at Warm Springs from 1924 through 1928, Alice Plastridge said, was that "he learned to use what he had—the good muscles. He learned another way of moving, which is really all you can expect, usually, several years after the onset of polio."

Mary Veeder put it this way: "If you don't get it [muscle development] back the first year or so, you don't get it back. He had poor to fair muscles [in 1928] and could only hope to maintain that. Maybe only poor to poor. He didn't really have any muscles at all. He walked on sheer determination."

Those views reflect an opposite view of Roosevelt's status than Dr. Hubbard is said to have had. Dr. Richard Goldberg, a psychologist, went into this in detail in a 1976 investigation of the effects of Roosevelt's polio on his personality. He concluded that Roosevelt had reached the limit of physical comeback in 1928, and therefore did not, in choosing to reenter politics, sacrifice an opportunity to walk. Even taking this view, and it seems to be the consensus view today, it still has to be said that Roosevelt thought he was on the threshold of regaining the ability to walk unaided, at least in a limited way, when he agreed to reenter active political life. His mail in this period demonstrates that. Letter after letter went forth in which he told friends, acquaintances, or perfect strangers who had inquired, that he would soon be able to "throw away crutches and canes," or similar optimistic locution. He may have thought his duties as governor would not interfere.

One of the most revealing letters of this period also

showed his good-humored reaction to his fame as a man with an infirmity. On December 2, 1928, Charles Ritz of Rochester wrote Roosevelt on the stationery of his firm, "Ritz Mfg. Co., Arch Supports and Foot Appliances." He asked the following questions:

"Can you walk without a cain or some assistants?

"Does both your shoes fit you even?

"Are you inclined to have a weakness also in the ankle?

"Are you sure of your step?

"Have you any pain below the hips? If so tell me where. . . ."

Roosevelt responded around the margin and across the bottom of the letter, with lines connecting his comments to the questions:

To the first question, he wrote, "Ans.—I cannot walk without a CAIN because I am not ABEL."

To the second, "Ans.—They fit me EVEN unless by accident I put on an ODD shoe—Ha Ha."

To the third, "Ans.—I have my little weakness like anybody else (Rotten)."

To the fourth, "Ans.—We all have to watch our step with so many prohibition agents around. (Not so good)."

To the fifth, "Ans.—My principal pain is in the neck when I get letters like this—(That will hold him)."

To all this Roosevelt added a thought to Missy LeHand, "(This is very subtle, but perhaps you can get *Punch* to print it.)"

Then he dictated the real reply:

"My dear Mr. Ritz:—

"Thank you for your letter of December 2nd. The answers are very simple, for I walk with either a crutch and cane or a cane and somebody's arm; both of my shoes fit me evenly, and I am not inclined to weakness in the ankle, and I am sure of my step; finally, I have no pain anywhere. It is still necessary for me to wear braces, but the leg muscles are gaining rapidly so that I hope eventually to get rid of them both."

On another occasion Roosevelt indicated that he could view his prognosis with humorous realism. He asked his wife in 1928 if she thought his reentry into politics would affect his health. She said all she could do was repeat what the doctors said—that if he devoted enough time to his exercising, he might improve. Roosevelt said that if he lived long enough he might indeed walk. He laughed when he said it, the implication being that that would take a long, long life.

In terms of comfort, Roosevelt undoubtedly made a great sacrifice in becoming governor. He continued to visit Georgia in the next four years for relaxation and therapy; he even made political use of the need for such trips. That is, he would go to Georgia to avoid having to make Hobson's Choice decisions. He wrote Howe in 1929, "When I am out of the state I possess no authority to act as governor." The lieutenant governor, Herbert Lehman, became acting governor. In the 1929 New York City mayoralty campaign, Roosevelt went to Georgia to avoid having to defend the Democratic candidate, incumbent Jimmy Walker, about whom the aroma of corruption and ineffectiveness was rising. Republican candidate Fiorello LaGuardia had a good issue to use against the Democrats when gambler Arnold Rothstein was murdered. He demanded a state investigation, the granting of which would have embarrassed

Walker, and the refusal of which could have come back to embarrass a national candidate later. So Roosevelt went south and left it up to Lehman.

Had Roosevelt turned Al Smith down and spent the next several years in undemanding endeavors, making more frequent trips to Warm Springs, his health in general and his legs would have benefited somewhat and *may* have benefited a great deal. So his decision was a sacrifice in a sense. But in what way would such a choice of life-style differ from what his mother had recommended in 1921? She wanted him to withdraw from professional life to Hyde Park, live the life of a retired gentleman. Isn't that what he would have been doing in Warm Springs? For a man like Roosevelt to give up a full political career, for whatever reason, for whatever gain, would have been self-invaliding. His legs would have become stronger and he would have become more of a cripple.

In 1927, Roosevelt spent 150 days in Warm Springs on four separate trips. He visited there six times in 1928, spending a total of 114 days. But in 1929, he was there only 61 days on three trips. In 1930, he went down only twice, for 53 days. In 1931, he made two trips that added up to 34 days. In 1932, when he was governor and the presidential nominee of his party, he got to Warm Springs for four weeks in the spring, a day in October, and for two weeks later. He never spent that much time there again.

The October visit was a campaign excursion. Roosevelt the candidate spoke in a setting that called attention to his affliction. But that affliction did not become an issue in the campaign—except in a positive, vote-winning, confidence-inspiring way.

*The Key Man*

*A note on sources for this chapter*

In addition to previously mentioned sources, *A Career in Progressive Democracy* by Ernest K. Lindley and *Franklin D. Roosevelt as Governor of New York* by Bernard Bellush were used. So was Elliott Roosevelt's *The Roosevelts of Hyde Park*, written with James Brough. Roosevelt's official papers and speeches, some collected and edited by Samuel Rosenman, others on file at the Roosevelt Library, were used here and in the following chapters.

# The Health Issue

The idea of a cripple in a physically demanding leadership role raises certain questions. "Is the individual able to meet the demands of his job?" is the most obvious. Roosevelt's instincts as a politician warned him from the earliest days—hours, in fact—of his affliction to be careful about the public's knowledge of his health. When he had been transferred from Campobello Island to the mainland en route to treatment in New York in 1921, flat on his back on a stretcher, Roosevelt and his political adviser Louis Howe both felt it was imperative that he not be seen in so helpless a posture. They connived to make the passage in secret. They improvised a stretcher rather than get one from the hospital in Eastport, for fear of tipping off reporters. Howe passed the word that Roosevelt would catch the train later in the day than he intended to. Howe also misinformed reporters as to which dock Roosevelt would land at on the mainland. As a result, no one saw Roosevelt flat on his back, and no one wrote stories speculating that he was extremely ill.

Roosevelt developed a number of ways to distract public attention from his inability to walk. He designed and insisted on armless wheelchairs, from and to which it was easier to move swiftly and smoothly to cars or other chairs. He learned that seven-passenger open cars were ideal for his purposes. In private, he was playful about his transfers into limousines. He would allow one of his New York State Trooper guards—Gus Gennerich or Earl Miller—to lift him with one strong arm under his limp legs and the other across his back. He would relax, almost go limp, with one arm around the shoulder of his bearer. Just as he was swung over the seat of the car, he might suddenly apply a viselike grip to the trooper's neck—his years of torso exercises had given him a wrestler's strength—and wrestle him into the car with him for a bit of awkward, boisterous horseplay. On other occasions he might yell "alley-oop" (or the trooper might) and allow himself to be literally tossed across a short space onto the seat. That was in private.

He was always dignified in public. Over the years, he got the transfer down pat. As Michael Reilly of the Secret Service described it, he would turn his back to the car and allow an agent to lift him from his wheelchair to a standing posture. He would reach backward and grasp the car door with both hands "and then he'd actually surge out of your arms" first to the jump seat then to the rear one. "He did this with such speed and grace that literally thousands who saw him at ball games, rallies and inaugurations never suspected his condition." Such large, open autos were not always easy to find in every place Roosevelt visited after he became President. Colonel Starling of the Secret Service once had to commandeer a fire department limousine in Dallas—and paint over its red body with black paint in a hurry.

Many did suspect his condition, from the time he ran for governor in 1928. It was never much of an issue, but it came up. Republicans raised it that year in the fashion of asking if he were up to the job's demands. Roosevelt prepared but did not use this reply: ". . . my only physical disability, which is a certain clumsiness in locomotion and which I trust will eventually disappear, has interfered in no way with my powers to think. Possibly because I find it more convenient to sit at my desk than to move around, I pride myself that during the past few years, I have done rather more than the average man's daily stint."

The *New York Post* said in an editorial that dwelt on his handicap, ". . . even his own friends out of love for him will hesitate to vote for him now." To which Roosevelt replied, "Nonsense . . . not only do I want my friends to vote for me, but if they are my real friends, I ask them to get as many other people to vote for me as possible." Roosevelt addressed the issue in one campaign speech, at Troy on October 26. "You know, I have been a little bit amused during the last three weeks. I understand . . . there was a great deal of what might be called sob stuff among the Republican editorial writers in the state of New York. They said, 'Isn't it too bad that that unfortunate man has had to be drafted for the Governorship? Isn't it too bad that his health won't stand it?'

"We started off nearly two weeks ago from the city of New York, consisting of a caravan—a whole flock of people, candidates, the press, the stenographic force, etc. We started in Orange County and we went on through Sullivan, Delaware, Broome, Steuben, and so forth. . . . One day we covered 180 miles by automobile and made seven speeches. . . . We left Utica this morning, intending to have an easy day of it. We got to Herkimer, where we all made speeches;

then we expected to come through Schenectady, but when we got to Fonda, there were forty or fifty automobiles in line blocking the road, and we were literally kidnapped. It threw the whole schedule out. We were told that up in that neck of the woods, Gloversville, where in the past there had been two Democrats and sometimes three . . . there were two thousand people waiting for us on the street . . . so we changed our plans a little and went up to Gloversville . . . When we came on down we were kidnapped again. We got to Amsterdam. We expected to go through Amsterdam just as fast as the traffic cops would let us, but there were sixteen hundred people . . . waiting . . . so we gave a speech. And then for good measure, we just dropped into Schenectady and spoke there earlier in the evening, and now here we are in Troy. Too bad about this unfortunate sick man, isn't it?"

Roosevelt made 33 speeches in the period of October 16 through November 1. In addition, brief remarks such as those in Amsterdam totaled in the "scores," according to one biographer who focused on that period. "This arduous schedule made people forget that Roosevelt was crippled," he wrote. Actually, as the Troy speech showed, the schedule was intended not to make people forget but to persuade them that his lameness either did not exist or that it was inconsequential. Al Smith spoke to the point in a more direct way than Roosevelt ever did. "A governor does not have to be an acrobat. We do not elect him for his ability to do a double back flip or a handspring." Roosevelt and especially Howe always feared that part of the public *did* want a leader who was as physically able-bodied and impressive as he was mentally astute, as nimble of foot as he was of brain. A conscious or unconscious yearning for a symbol of masculinity in the state house or White House.

Roosevelt did a second thing to disarm the whispering critics of his health. He initiated and emphasized the issue of aid to cripples. In Rochester, on October 22, he said the state had both economic and humanitarian interests in restoring cripples to health. The former he based on one of his favorite arguments, that money spent to make cripples wage-earners would "come back many times through their increased productiveness." The latter he based on the need to make people able to live happily amidst their families and friends as "normal" people. "It is, of course, a fact that the family of the average cripple cannot afford to pay the heavy cost of obtaining proper private treatment, and we must come to a better realization that this care is as much a part of the duties of the local and state governments as it is for those governments to provide the funds for the development of the child's education. . . ."

In his remarks in behalf of this constituency, Roosevelt presented himself as a *cured* cripple. "I suppose that people readily recognize that I myself furnish a perfectly good example of what can be done by the right kind of care. I dislike to use this personal example, but it happens to fit. Seven years ago in the epidemic in New York, I came down with infantile paralysis, a perfectly normal attack, and I was completely, for the moment, put out of any useful activities. By personal good fortune I was able to get the very best kind of care, and the result of having the best kind of care is that today I am on my feet.

"And while I shall not vouch for the mental side of it, I am quite certain that from the physical point of view, I am quite capable of going to Albany and staying there two years." That line must have brought a wry smile to Louis Howe. He had insisted on describing Roosevelt's malady as a "heavy cold, threatening pneumonia" when his friend was first struck down. Why? "Because the word 'paralysis' has dire implications," he told Eleanor at the time. "There might be confusion in the public thought with meningitis, intimations that Franklin's mind had been affected. . . . It would be easy to create an impression that would wreck his political career." Seven years later his political career had him on the threshold of high office—and he was joking about his "mental" assets.

After he became governor, Roosevelt relaxed a little bit. Dr. Hubbard gave him some "rules." "Remain in bed until 9:30 A.M., doing your work while resting there from 9 A.M. on if you choose. Rest a full hour at noon, lying down for a short time. Exercise in warm water in a swimming pool as soon as that is possible. Keep away from frills, the endless round of hand-shaking and official dinners." Without mentioning the need for such limitation, Dr. Hubbard was quoted in the *New York Times* as saying that "the duties of a governor are arduous, but I think Mr. Roosevelt is up to them."

Roosevelt promptly began following Dr. Hubbard's advice about doing business in bed. He seemed to like it. He would continue to operate that way in the White House later, with such apparent relaxed pleasure that one adviser, Rexford Tugwell, would describe it as "regal" mannerism.

Once he became governor, Roosevelt followed up on his campaign rhetoric about aid to crippled children. He continued to stress both the moral obligation of society to the weak and also the "waste" of allowing crippled men and women to remain unproductive. (This was a theme he mentioned often in private, too.) In his first annual message to the New York Legislature in 1929, he said the state had the same obligation to help cripples walk as it did to help chil-

dren to read and write. He promised a program to that end.
Later that year he went on an inspection tour of state hospitals and schools. He said that while much had been done,
much more remained to be done. He said a big obstacle to
doing more was that the public was "ignorant" about the
situation. "This is a problem that demands a great cru-
sade," he said. He set up a commission he hoped would lead
to increased state activity, but the Republican legislature
was slow to react, and the 1932 presidential campaign eventually ended his efforts in that direction.

But these efforts did act to keep his health before the public. In April 1931, with the presidential talk swirling around
him, he was given an opportunity to face it head-on. An old
family friend, Earl Looker, proposed that he follow Roosevelt around in Albany for a few days. Three physicians
would also examine the Governor. After that, Looker would
write a report of the Governor's health and stamina for
*Liberty* magazine. Looker told his readers that he was a
Republican. The implication was that he would be very
objective, even critical. Roosevelt accepted with pleasure.
He knew, if Looker didn't (and Looker must have), that
seven months before, an objective if not critical physician
had found him in excellent health. In October 1930, he
had been examined for that $560,000 "key man" policy
Keith Morgan had arranged. The examination took place
in the Roosevelt home on East 65th Street. Roosevelt not
only got the policy, he got an endorsement. Dr. E. W. Beckwith, medical director of the Equitable Life Assurance Co.,
who conducted the examination, wrote him, "it has rarely
been my privilege as an examining physician for life insurance to see such a splendid physical specimen as yourself."

To reporters, Dr. Beckwith said, "Governor Roosevelt
was examined at the end of the week in which the [state

Democratic] convention was held. He has been under very great strain and it was an astonishing fact that his heart and blood pressure were absolutely normal. . . . I would say that his examination disclosed conditions which were comparable to a man of thirty." In addition to finding his vital signs youthful, the life insurance examination also volunteered the finding that Roosevelt's abdominal muscles were "entirely regenerated" and his thigh muscles "somewhat regenerated."

To that local publicity bonanza, the aspiring presidential candidate got the nationally circulated bonus from *Liberty*. In the July 25, 1931, issue Looker wrote a five-page article that began with this headline: "Is Franklin D. Roosevelt Fit To Be President?" Looker quoted his exchange of letters with Roosevelt. He described how he followed Roosevelt around the state capital and observed him at work. He quoted from the report of the three examining doctors chosen by a New York professional medical society—internist Samuel W. Lambert, orthopedist Russell A. Hibbs, neurologist Foster Kennedy—who found him able to do his job and progressively getting better physically. Looker concluded, "In fairness, then, to Franklin Roosevelt, let it be said that whether his traits of character indicate his fitness or his unfitness for the presidency, *he is physically fit*."

The conclusions about his ability to continue to gain strength were probably overstated. But the important thing was that the public was being told that the man was not an invalid. Public perception and misperception being what it is, even that might not have taken the issue out of a national campaign if Roosevelt had not perfected his public movements to hide the true nature of his crippled limbs. That is, a healthy man who cannot walk may not seem capable of leadership, while an unhealthy man who can walk would provide confidence. As mentioned earlier, Roosevelt knew that instinctively, and since 1921 had acted to provide a public picture of a man in control of all his faculties and powers.

In 1932, American voters desired confidence more than they had in most previous elections. The Depression that had begun in 1929 was the reason for that. Roosevelt went beyond offering confidence. He offered America inspiration. Far from hiding his history of infirmity, he used it as a confidence-builder. He did it in simple ways, like saying, as he did in one 1931 radio address, that his ailment was the sort that resulted in "the finest natural disposition." He was talking about "the average cripple," not about himself, so it was not a boast. But it served, in a minor way to be sure, to suggest that he would be a calm, unflustered leader in a time of frenzy. He could "keep his head when all about were losing theirs," to quote the sort of uplift poetry he liked. (He told an inquiring newspaper editor once that his favorite poem was William Ernest Henley's *Invictus*. "In the fell clutch of circumstance/I have not winced nor cried aloud. . . . I am master of my fate:/I am the captain of my soul.")

As the 1932 campaign began, there were again whispers about his health. Howe was told that some Republicans were going to charge that polio was a progressive disease that eventually affected the mind. Drs. Draper and Lovett prepared a rebuttal to that that was never used. Dr. Hubbard did write—or sign—a lengthy letter to the editor of the *New York Sun*, rebutting any and all charges. "Aside from the weakness of the muscles of his legs . . . he has been in perfect physical condition." He cited the life insurance policy "at the normal [premium] rate for his age," and added: "Insurance companies are cold blooded and have no sentiment in their business, and at the time the policy was issued, it was well known that he would probably be a candidate for the presidency."

Roosevelt presented an even more vigorous picture to the nation than he had to New Yorkers in 1928. Primaries were not important then as they would become after World War II. Roosevelt made a few speeches and a very few trips out of New York before he won the nomination at the Chicago convention in July. He took the unprecedented step of flying to the convention to accept the nomination. That symbolism of a man on the move was maintained until the election. After a handful of speeches in July and August, Roosevelt embarked on an eight-week continent-spanning campaign, in which he made 83 speeches.

One of the briefest speeches he made was to his adoring companions at Warm Springs on October 23. He made a special trip there from Atlanta, sandwiching the visit between two Atlanta addresses on the 23rd and 24th. The patients and staff, led by Fred Botts in a battered silk top hat, greeted him with a small parade. They led him to the front of the hospital. Many young patients were seated in a circle on the grounds. Others were on the porch of the hospital. Roosevelt did not leave his car. "Two more weeks to go," he said, to applause. ". . . First, let me say this: This old hat, a lot of you people have seen it before. It's the same hat. But I don't think it is going to last much longer after the 8th of November. [Laughter, applause] I have a superstition about hats in campaigns, and I am going to wear it until midnight of the 8th of November. [Applause] . . . Well, it's fine to see, and I am looking forward to coming down here for the usual Thanksgiving party at Warm Springs, and having a real old-fashioned Thanksgiving with my neighbors again. I thank you!" (Applause)

He could have said anything and won their applause. To them he was a great symbol of triumph, however his political fortunes turned out. As Frances Perkins, who would become his Labor Secretary, put it, "His relations with the other patients at Warm Springs . . . were interesting and charming to see. He was one of them—he was a big brother —he had been through it—he was smiling—he was courageous—he was feeling fine—he encouraged you to try—he said you could do it. 'I did it, you can too,' was his attitude." Mary Veeder, the physiotherapist, who saw the reaction of the other patients day in and day out for years, said, "He inspired them *all*. If he'd never done anything but this, he'd be a great humanitarian." Even in the midst of a campaign, Roosevelt knew this and apparently attached some importance to it. Why else the long campaign detour from Atlanta to Warm Springs and back?

Even after he became President, he continued to accept his responsibility as symbol of conqueror of disease. One day in the fall of 1935, while in Georgia for Thanksgiving, he came to visit some patients at a Sunday evening devotional. General Evans Carlson later described the scene in a letter to Missy LeHand. "We had placed a chair at the roadside for the President's use, but when he drove up he waved the chair aside. Descending from the car, he drew himself up, and with magnificent dignity and superb will, he walked down the ramp through the door and forward to his seat amid the patients. Never will I forget that walk, which was performed in utter silence. No explanation was ever given for what must have been a supreme effort. But I sensed, and I felt that others present must have sensed, that it was made for the purpose of giving hope and inspiration to the assembled patients."

Such displays of determination were inspiring to healthy

Americans as well—those who recognized him as a symbol of recovery from another kind of paralysis. This was surely not conscious in most cases. But the fact was that at a time of economic paralysis and fear, a man who had conquered physical paralysis and fear—one way or another—was now offering himself as a leader to conquer that other kind. He used just such language in his acceptance speech, specifically the word "paralysis" to describe the Depression's effects. The word was not often used in such a context before 1932. And though Roosevelt was not the only one to use it, it is nonetheless interesting to note that the edition of *Webster's New World International Dictionary* then in use gave only the medical context of the word "paralysis," while the next edition to appear gave the fuller description applied today. Roosevelt made "paralysis" a metaphor for economic depression.

Roosevelt and his speechwriters often used variations on this metaphor in the years ahead. For example, in 1936 he complained that some of the "sick patients of 1932" were cured to the point that they could "throw their crutches at the doctor." Dr. Roosevelt of the Warm Springs pool had become Dr. Roosevelt to a limping nation. Dr. New Deal he called himself. In 1937 Roosevelt talked of "quarantining" aggressive dictatorships. And in 1941, in another attack on such governments, he interwove two themes: "We are still living under a free people's philosophy. . . . We believe in and insist on the right of the helpless, the right of the weak, and the right of the crippled everywhere to play their part in life—and survive." This was an appeal for funds to combat infantile paralysis, but Roosevelt made it clear he was talking about the right of weak *nations* also. In a 1944 appeal for funds, he said, "The dread disease that we battle at home, like the enemy we oppose abroad. . . ." When war became his central concern, he ceased being "Old Dr. New Deal" and became "Dr. Win the War." He described the former as an internist and the latter as an orthopedic surgeon, by the way.

Roosevelt also liked to use figures of speech that conjured up mental pictures of physical prowess. In a 1939 radio address, for example, he said this about political types: "I am reminded of four definitions: A radical is a man with both feet planted firmly—in the air. A conservative is a man with two perfectly good legs who, however, has never learned to walk forward. A reactionary is a somnambulist walking backwards. A liberal is a man who uses his legs and his hands at the behest—at the command—of his head." Roosevelt, of course, was a liberal.

(In thought but not always in deed Roosevelt was a liberal when it came to health-care issues. He thought the federal role could be and should be large. But he never pushed this too far. In 1934 he set up a special committee to study and devise an economic security system. Among its ideas was health insurance. Roosevelt said at that time that he thought "sooner or later" some sort of insurance plan would be adopted. The Social Security Act that was enacted the next year did not deal with health insurance, but it did provide $8,000,000 for the Public Health Service to assist state and local governments with their medical programs. This was increased to $11,000,000 in 1939. Also in 1939, the health insurance issue came up again; a special high-level cabinet group had proposed it among other changes in the economic security, welfare and health field. Roosevelt passed the recommendation on to Congress. Bitter opposition came from conservatives and, especially, from the American Medical Association. Some of Roosevelt's aides understood him to say health insurance would be the big domestic issue in 1940. They expected him to stick by the recommendation. But he didn't. He withdrew his support of national health insurance legislation, while insisting that it was not socialized medicine. He supported only a bill that would provide federal funds for the WPA, a program of federally sponsored employment projects during the Depression, to build hospitals in poor rural areas. It may be that his personal experience with physicians, which for the most part had been quite good, created in him a respect for their independence that tempered his liberalism on the health insurance issue. The hospitals program certainly reflected his rural experiences. What he had in mind, he said, were painted frame buildings that would only cost $150,000 including all equipment.)

In 1932, at least, the public certainly perceived Roosevelt as a vigorous male animal. It is unlikely that his political opponents could have made much headway with attacks on his health. Howe and others had made sure that there was plenty of publicity portraying Roosevelt on the go. Some of it was contrived. He had taken up horseback riding shortly after he began going to Warm Springs. He liked to ride. The rustic resort had no paved roads for autos and many of the dirt trails and, later, bridle paths permitted riding but not driving. He was a good horseman, but his thigh weakness made it difficult and unrelaxing. He did not ride after about 1928, according to contemporaries at Warm Springs—except when there were photographers around. There often were in 1931 and 1932. Every big newspaper library had photographs of FDR astride a horse.

Another form of physical activity that his leg muscle weakness was a liability in was deep-sea fishing. But in that, at least, his great shoulder and arm strength compensated. Roosevelt truly loved fishing and continued to do it the rest of his life. Voters in 1932—and later—were treated to pictures of him in the stern chair of deep-sea fishing boats and on docks with large game fish he had landed. He was also a very physical swimmer, if not a graceful one. His stroke was described as "modified Australian crawl," but it could just as easily have been called a "modified dog paddle." But still pictures and newsreels of him in the pool at Warm Springs—playing water football, never doing therapeutic exercises—showed him strong and aggressive. He also liked to sail. The public was treated to many pictures of him at the helm of sailing craft. One of his earliest vacations after he became President was as captain of a sailing ship. The symbolism of the skipper was obvious, but the other symbols of an active athlete were just as effective: swimming perhaps more so, since it was a more obvious reminder that Roosevelt was not only strong but that his strength was *regained* strength.

Many Americans had no idea that Roosevelt was dependent on braces, crutches, canes and strong arms. During his 1932 campaign by train, he had a special long ramp with steady hand rails constructed to allow him to walk up and down a relatively gentle incline. Some spectators occasionally expressed surprise at how slowly Roosevelt walked. But they saw a man who walked—and walked alone. At many stops, Roosevelt did not leave the train. Usually, he was already standing on the rear platform of the train when it chugged slowly into the station. He would speak briefly at such stops. He'd stand, waving farewell, as the train departed. Back on the road he would allow Gus Gennerich, his personal bodyguard, to help him into the car. There

McDuffie, his valet, would remove his pants and braces. He'd put his pants back on and relax. He had found much lighter braces by 1931. They weighed about three pounds each, compared to the seven pounds each of those he wore before then. But they were still uncomfortable.

People who knew about Roosevelt's infirmity were as impressed by his appearance as those who did not know. Some, like Josephus Daniels, who was Roosevelt's boss as Secretary of the Navy during World War I, saw a more complex symbol in his old protégé than the one so far described. He compared him to the world, "which had been so strong, so beautiful" in that period before the war, and then was "crippled with the paralysis of bitterness" in 1921.

He did not mean that *Roosevelt* became a bitter man. Almost everyone who ever had close contacts with Roosevelt over the last quarter-century of his life was struck by his lack of bitterness, his cheery personality.  This is a characteristic of many, though hardly all, polios. Admiral Ross McIntire, Roosevelt's physician after he became President, found him to have the most healthy personality he had encountered. Mabel Irwin, the wife of a surgeon at Warm Springs, a close social friend of Roosevelt, said after his death she *"never"* saw him depressed, never saw him sad.

According to one biographer, Jean Gould, who interviewed Eleanor Roosevelt on the subject of Roosevelt's mental and emotional reaction to his polio, a rare display of bitterness (after the depressed reaction immediately following the onset of the disease) came in the mid-1920s, when his friend John Lawrence and he were considering buying a houseboat. "Well, I might as well write Johnny to go ahead; at least that way I won't be a burden to anyone!" Miss Gould quotes him as saying to Eleanor.

Elliott Roosevelt said in later years he never saw his father depressed. James wrote that he saw him display a lack of self-confidence once and only once. That was the night he was elected President. James helped him into bed on 65th Street. Roosevelt said he'd never been afraid of anything till then. "I'm afraid I may not have the strength to do the job." He prayed for strength.

In the White House Roosevelt's emotional equilibrium never failed him. "Sometimes he would revolt against his wheelchair and the fate that had put him there," wrote White House seamstress and maid Lillian Park Rogers. "Then he would complain and become irritable. At such times there was only one thing to do—give him a rubdown to soothe his weary, wasted muscles and relax his mind." Miss Rogers was one of the two polios on the White House staff. She had been there when Hoover was President. Antoinette Bachelder, a Warm Springs acquaintance of Roosevelt's, came after Roosevelt moved in. The President's rare moody revolts were never seen by the public, or even suspected, it appears. He knew the importance of a leader's displaying his sunny side in a dark era. Either by force of will or simple chemistry of personality, the moods passed quickly, anyway.

Walter Trohan, the White House correspondent for the *Chicago Tribune*, understood how Roosevelt's leadership qualities were obvious at a glance. "Although he could not walk, he had the face of a marching man. His chin was tilted high in confidence, his eyes were bright with purpose, and his spirits were gay." The newspaper publisher Dorothy Schiff, who became a frequent companion of Roosevelt's, also was inspired by that quality of confidence. She drew inspiration and strength from him. She once rushed from a meeting with him to her psychiatrist, Harry Stack Sullivan, to describe Roosevelt as "radiant." James Farley, Roosevelt's campaign manager in 1932, wrote later that "he was the most alive man I had ever met . . . when he talked, he emphasized his points with sharp gestures and constant changes of facial expressions. He would have been a great actor."

Such qualities, and especially such behavior, tended to distract audiences and intimates from Roosevelt's handicap. As newspaper reporter Ernest K. Lindley put it, "The thing about Roosevelt that necessarily strikes you when you see him walking the first time is the thing about him of which you first become unconscious." He mesmerized people, to the extent that they thought of him as a physically sound man. "Don't get up," Madame Chiang Kai-shek said, without thinking, on leaving the White House one evening.

He would have been a great actor. That is almost certainly what he was when he jutted his chin, shrugged his shoulders, fluttered his hands, arched his eyebrows, elevated his cigarette holder, and so forth. There is another school of thought to the effect that polios with useless legs compensate for inability to move about normally with exaggerated motions of hands, arms, shoulders, face. But Dr. Stuart Raper, an orthopedic surgeon who came to Warm Springs in the 1930s and got to know Roosevelt, says that is not an automatic reaction. It was not natural for Roosevelt to so project himself. He learned it. It was probably quite a complicated learning task. Edward Herrmann, the actor who portrayed Roosevelt in two television dramas in the 1970s, studied many old newsreels and home movies to learn dozens of Roosevelt's different gestures. Not one was a "natural" way to express an emotion or a point. Roosevelt had developed a repertoire and was careful not to overwork any single gesture. That jutted jaw and clenched cigarette holder came to be regarded as a cliché, but otherwise Roosevelt was a careful, thoughtful actor who knew how not to bore his audience with predictable bits of "business" or cause his audience to mistrust his gestures and postures.

Did Roosevelt learn other things from his polio? Eleanor Roosevelt believed he learned "the greatest of all lessons—infinite patience and never-ending persistence." She said his illness gave him "strength and courage he had not had before" and made him "more aware of the feelings of people." People who had known him less well, before and after, and people who had not known him at all before, observed what they took to be benefits from his illness. Colonel Edmund Starling, chief of the White House Secret Service detail in 1932, said of Roosevelt after watching him on Inauguration Day, "I realized he had somehow overcome more than a physical illness. He had somehow acquired a vigor, an optimism, a feeling of sureness in himself which he had never before possessed." Starling had had no experience with Roosevelt, but he had had experience with another crippled President, Woodrow Wilson, who suffered a stroke in the White House. Wilson, Starling wrote, reacted with bad temper and pettiness to his misfortune, in marked contrast to Roosevelt.

In a profile of Roosevelt for the *New York Times* in March 1933, Anne O'Hare McCormack wrote, "A friend of Hoover, an astute judge of men who has known Roosevelt since the days of the Wilson administration, commented on the change in the new President. 'Two years ago I saw Roosevelt after a long interval. Today I saw him again. He is no more like the man who was here in Wilson's time than the capital is like the city it was then. He has developed in all directions, far beyond what seemed his natural capacity. I attribute the change to his physical disability. Having overcome that, he is not afraid of anything. The daily course in self-discipline and self-control has strengthened his will, tempered his character; in his years of enforced inactivity, he became a student and a thinker. Part of the power of the first Roosevelt was that he conquered physical weakness. This man functions smoothly because he has learned to function in chains.' "

Eleanor again: The illness was "a blessing in disguise."

The forced associations which Roosevelt's illness brought about proved to be a valuable learning experience for him in many ways, of course, but one way he identified himself has often been overlooked. Listen to what he had to say in a tribute to the Mayo brothers, Will and Charles. "Those of us who are concerned with the problems of government and of economics are under special obligation to modern medicine in two very important respects. In the first place, it has taught us that with patience and application and skill and courage it is possible for human beings to control and improve conditions under which they live. It has taught us how science may be made the servant of a richer, more complete common life. And it has taught us more than that, because from it we have learned lessons in the ethics of human relationships—how devotion to the public good, unselfish service, never-ending consideration of human needs are in themselves conquering forces." How fortunate the nation was, when optimism or at least hope was so desirable, that its President in the depths of the Depression was the sort of person who drew such lessons from a long and not wholly satisfactory partnership with medical science to cure a disabling condition.

In other, lesser ways Roosevelt's affliction might have been a blessing to him. The *New York Evening World* said of him once that "adversity has lifted him above the bickering." He seemed somehow ungrasping and unselfish. Contrast that with how he would have been perceived in 1924 and 1928 if he had still been the handsome, youthful, wealthy, unmarked New Yorker he was before he contracted polio. He would still have been an imposing figure; though hardly what he became. He might even have been his party's nominee for President in 1924 and again in 1928. And if he had? *No* Democrat could have been elected President in either of those years. Roosevelt would surely have lost, and in 1932 would the party have turned to a two-time loser? Probably not.

There is still another "if" approach to this history. Roosevelt could not have been nominated in 1924, 1928 or even 1932 without his affliction. The Democratic party had not nominated a wealthy aristocrat (though it had chosen self-made wealthy men) in the century after Jackson made it the true party of the common man. Polio, as it has been put, was Roosevelt's log cabin.

Finally, there was another sort of symbolism involved in Roosevelt's disease and recovery. To many people of fundamentalist religions in Georgia, he was thought of as a participant in a drama of religious content. W. G. Harry, a minister and the mayor of Warm Springs in the 1930s, thought about this at length. He wrote a book about Roosevelt in which he talked about his mission to be the "deliverance" of the poor of the earth. He saw Warm Springs as a "desert experience" for Roosevelt. The Roosevelt cottage at Warm Springs was a "literal wilderness." Roosevelt's first immersion in the mineral waters of Warm Springs was a "baptism" that allowed Roosevelt to be born again. Roosevelt drew strength and wisdom from the "mount of meditation." He is destined to live in history because he moved among the plain people, "as Jesus did." Another Warm Springs resident saw him as only slightly less exalted. "I tell you what I always call him. I call him the second Moses. Moses led the children out of Israel and he led us out of a depression," said Mrs. Sam Killian. Well, there is no getting around the fact that Roosevelt did lead the country out of the Depression. And he did move among the plain people. At least in Meriwether County, Georgia, he did.

## *A note on sources for this chapter*

In addition to previously cited books, and in addition to interviews, the following secondary sources were also helpful here and throughout this book: *This I Remember* and *This Is My Story* by Eleanor Roosevelt, *The Roosevelt I Knew* by Frances Perkins, *Starling of the White House* by Colonel Edmund Starling as told to Thomas Sugrue, *Reilly of the White House* by Michael Reilly as told to William Slocum, *Working with Roosevelt* by Samuel Rosenman, *Behind the Ballots* by James Farley, *Franklin D. Roosevelt* by Alden Hatch, *Roosevelt in Retrospect* by John Gunther. *My Thirty Years Backstairs at the White House* by Lillian Rogers Parks in collaboration with Frances Spatz Leighton.

# *At Home in a God-Forsaken Region*

---

The Warm Springs Roosevelt came to in 1924 was quite unlike the small-town and rural Hudson River Valley area he knew best. The Great Depression was still five years away for most of the nation. The Roaring '20s were accelerating toward the brink elsewhere. But in Meriwether County and much of the South hard times had come about the time Roosevelt suffered his polio attack. The area's economy depended on cotton. The world war had brought about a boom for cotton farmers. In New Orleans just after the end of the war, cotton sold for over 40 cents a pound. In a few months the price fell to a third of that figure. Another Deep South money crop, tobacco, fell about 50 percent in price. Thereafter, the rural South was in the grips of its own depression. In Meriwether County, where cotton had always been an important crop, the impact was typical. Farmers kept planting cotton, as the price fluctuated from about a dime to a quarter a pound in the '20s. The low price, plus the onslaught of the boll weevil, which ruined the cotton bolls and thus reduced the yield, meant that farmers were getting little in return for small crops. There were some attempts at diversification, particularly in peaches, but these, too, provided little cash income.

The town of Warm Springs and the surrounding countryside reflected this poverty in physical scenery as well as in social statistics and mores. The paved road from Atlanta ended in Greenville, about a dozen miles away. The town was a mixture of a few well-maintained homes, many run-down houses, a squalid black slum, a small business district. The countryside was even more poverty-stricken. Barns sagged, were unpainted, often had rusted corrugated metal patches on walls and roofs. There were no lawns around farmhouses, merely well-worn hard-packed red clay "yards." The houses themselves were small—three or four rooms—with neither glass windows nor screens. Many of the farms were usually worked by sharecroppers. It was a hard life for almost all concerned. The farms were not mechanized. Planting, harvesting and maintenance were done with the aid of mules and black field hands. Often, even the mule was rented. "Dollar and a half a day for a mule, dollar and a half a day for a nigger," as one farmer summed it up.

Rex Tugwell, who came down from New York to visit Roosevelt later, remarked that the southern drawls and language were "strange." Certainly the mores and the suffocating poverty were strange, too. Eleanor suffered culture shock. Even at the somewhat better-maintained resort area in the first few years the Roosevelts went to Georgia, conditions were almost primitive. "You could see daylight through the cracks in the wall [of the Hart cottage]," Eleanor said. Local stores were not prepared to fill some of the requests for food. "Steaks, broccoli, we never knew that," a merchant complained. So the Roosevelts accommodated themselves to the local delights. That was not without its charm, particularly for the inquisitive Franklin, and even for Eleanor. In an interview years later she said, "The people were so kind, and keeping house was one of the amusing things when we started, because we discovered that for the most part we had to buy things like chickens on the hoof—and chickens were the main things you could buy to eat, so we would come back [to the Hart cottage or the cottage Roosevelt subsequently built nearby] after having driven to some nearby town with three or four chickens tied by their legs in the back of the car, and then let them loose and they would wander 'round until the cook would go out and catch one, among many squeaks, and would wring its neck. . . . I never liked that idea very much. . . . It was . . . too personal to eat it."

The local milk and cream, as Roosevelt later told a press conference, "was not certified . . . it was not what you would call from inspected dairies." There was definitely a sense of roughing it at times. There were radio stations in Atlanta and some other southern cities in the '20s, but reception was so staticky that Roosevelt seldom took advantage of it. Electricity was available, but on a somewhat erratic basis in the early years. When the Warm Springs Foundation got an X-ray machine, it had to alert the power company in Manchester when it planned to use it, to make sure there was enough power available. Most of the farm homes had no electric appliances. Those that did used battery systems which had to be cranked often to keep lights on.

Henry Wallace, Secretary of Agriculture, got his first look at the rural Southeast after Roosevelt was elected President. The Iowan was shocked by what he saw. "I was utterly amazed and appalled at the red-gashed hillsides, at the unkempt cabins . . . what a God-forsaken region it appeared to be."

Other visitors from outside the region had the same reaction. The scene must have looked as strange to Roosevelt, but it never seemed to repulse him. He seemed to fit right in. One reason for that may have been that in a few significant ways, the Meriwether County of the late 1920s was similar to the Dutchess County of the early years of the century. For example, they both supported Prohibition and opposed both Sunday baseball and spending much money on teacher salaries.

That dollar-and-a-half-a-day pay for a black field hand was not even a bottom figure. Roosevelt later bought a farm in the county. His 1928 records show "one man 2 days harrowing" for $3 and "one boy hoeing trees for 8 hours" for 45 cents. And some of the local farm owners complained in those days that Roosevelt paid too much for help. "He paid New York wages," a farmer there said.

Roosevelt liked to drive around that blasted-looking landscape that so repelled others from more favored regions. It wasn't that he liked it as it was, but that he had a great desire to improve things. It was certainly ripe for that. At first his trips to town and over country roads to Manchester and Greenville and other nearby towns were as a passenger in someone else's automobile. He wanted more freedom than that. He sketched a set of hand controls for an auto that would allow him to work clutch, brake and accelerator despite his lameness. A local mechanic named Ponder bought for Roosevelt an old Model T Ford about ten years old, with canvas top, high body, wooden spoked wheels, and adapted it to Roosevelt's design. It was widely reported that the car cost $50. About a week after Roosevelt gave him the design, Ponder drove up to the Roosevelt cottage near the inn. FDR came out in his wheelchair. He clicked his braces, stood up and backed into the passenger seat. Ponder drove slowly around the area, as Roosevelt watched the operation of the hand controls. About a mile out of town, Roosevelt said he was ready to take over. He drove at a very fast—for him then—25 miles per hour, through the town of Warm Springs and on over to Manchester and back. In Warm Springs he stopped at the curb in front of the drugstore and yelled, "Let's have a Coke!" When served, he boasted, "How do you like my new car? It's the latest model."

Thereafter, he always had a hand-controlled auto at Warm Springs (and at Hyde Park). He replaced the Model T with a new Model A when it appeared in 1929. He later switched to other models.

With his freedom thus gained, Roosevelt began to explore his adopted home. He became "almost as familiar to the agrarian population as the rural mail carrier," as a resident there recalled it. "There was this difference, the mail carrier did take Sunday off." On Sunday, the Episcopal vestryman from the Hudson Valley would occasionally drop by one of the two churches in town: One was Baptist and one Methodist. Those were social visits. But for the most part, his forays were educational tours.

One Roosevelt visit to a farm has been reconstructed by a contemporary:

ROOSEVELT: "Who is your landlord? Where does he live?"
SHARECROPPER: "De landlord is ................... He lives in town."

ROOSEVELT: "What is his occupation?"

SHARECROPPER: "He has a store in Manchester."

ROOSEVELT: "How many cows do you have? How many chickens? How many hogs?"

SHARECROPPER: "No, sir; we don't keep er cow. We jus have one hog. De possums and de weasels and de foxes eats up de chickens so bad dat we just don't bother with 'em."

ROOSEVELT: "What do you raise on your farm?"

SHARECROPPER: "We jus raise cotton and corn on de farm."

ROOSEVELT: "How much cotton did you gather last year?"

SHARECROPPER: "We raise two bales er cotton dis year. De boll weevil wuz might bad dis time. Las year we raise five bales, but de boll wevil wuz not so bad las year."

ROOSEVELT: "Do you have a garden?"

SHARECROPPER: "De cotton keeps us so busy we don't have time to bother with a garden. We jus have a little patch of collard greens."

ROOSEVELT: "How many children do you have?"

SHARECROPPER: "We has six children."

ROOSEVELT: "Do your children go to school?"

SHARECROPPER: "No, sir; none of de children go ter school. Dey don't have no shoes and purty clothes to wear, so dey jus stay home and helps me and der mama."

ROOSEVELT: "Why don't you put a new roof on your house?"

SHARECROPPER: "I tol de landlord if he buy de tin I put it on. He say de land don't pay nuff so he afford to buy de tin. We jus move de table and de beds round when it rains to dry spots."

Though the interview that reconstruction was based on

was with black sharecroppers, the interviewer added that "the answers [FDR] received from the white sharecroppers to the same questions were identical."

According to some who recall those years, Roosevelt did not approach this educational task in a bullying manner. Such questions did not spill out in a rapid-fire third degree. Rather, he chatted with his neighbors. He got to know them by name. "He was always the squire," one Georgian reminisced later, "but he was genuinely liked and seemed to like everybody." At Hyde Park he was a Roosevelt, scion of a wealthy, socially prominent family, with all the baggage that implied, but at Warm Springs he was just a rich politician from far away who was trying to make friends. And succeeding.

He made friends in the town and the countryside, in addition to the separate set of people he became close to through the Georgia Warm Springs Foundation. There was a "town and gown" sort of separateness there, but Roosevelt moved back and forth between the two communities with ease. He soon knew almost everybody. Sam Killian owned a store in town. On several occasions in the years before he became President, Roosevelt would call him at night from his cottage, Mrs. Killian recalled later, and the conversation would go something like this: "Mrs. Killian, is Sam there?"

"Yes, sir."

"May I speak to him? What are you doing, Sam? You real busy? How about coming over for a little confab?"

It was not just Killian, Mrs. Killian said. "You see, he wanted to learn every figure in this town by their first name. And he'd call 'em. He wanted to *know every* white person. He really, truly was a neighbor."

Roosevelt never undertook to remonstrate with his white Georgian neighbors about the evils of the racist arrangement of their society, except in indirect ways. For one thing, he probably knew there wasn't anything he could do. For another, Georgia was a place for *relaxing* as well as everything else, and he just didn't want the hassle. And for another, he always knew that his political fortunes, in terms of becoming President and then in terms of getting what he wanted as President, depended in large part on good relations with southern members of Congress. So he left that to Eleanor.

Eleanor began asking questions about the plight of black Georgians in the car riding from the train station to the Hart cottage the first night the Roosevelts arrived in Warm Springs. She never stopped. At least according to local memories. Fifty years later—thirty years after Roosevelt's death—some elderly local white ladies still recalled Eleanor's visits to the area with something less than affection. The wife of a leading Manchester merchant of the 1920s and 1930s summed it up most succinctly. "We didn't like her a bit," she said softly in an interview. She paused and gazed down the residential street as if she were gazing back through time. She sighed and said with feeling but not bitterness, "She ruined every maid we ever had."

What Roosevelt did do from the beginning was challenge his new friends' views on a somewhat related issue—that of anti-Catholicism. In a circumspect and neighborly way, of course. In the spring of 1925, on his second visit to Warm Springs, Roosevelt became a temporary newspaper columnist. Tom Loyless wrote for the *Macon Telegraph*. He was ill, and hard pressed in his efforts to make improvements on the Meriwether Inn that spring. He asked Roosevelt to pinch-hit for him. Roosevelt wrote nine columns. One was titled "We Lack a Sense of Humor If We Forget That Not So Very Long Ago We Were Immigrants Ourselves." It was a gentle rebuke to nativist notions.

He wrote that "a certain agricultural county in a Northern state with which I am very familiar" had prided itself on its English, Scotch and Dutch bloodlines. He said the county became quite backward until south German and then northern Italian "peasants" moved in and led the way to prosperity. "Don't forget that some of the most backward and ignorant sections of the United States in the Northern and Southern states are populated almost exclusively with the so-called 'pure American stock.' "

Roosevelt also took it upon himself to campaign among his Georgia neighbors for Al Smith for President—in particular—and the civil rights of Catholics in general. Roosevelt liked to tell this story about his campaign. "One morning, when I was sound asleep, it was around daylight, about five o'clock, somebody banged on the shutters. . . . So I got into a little wheelchair and went over and opened the shutters and there was an old gentleman from over in Shiloh Valley.

"He said, 'Mr. Roosevelt . . . we are all upset about you . . . We people over in Shiloh Valley, we are sort of old-fashioned and we believe the written word.'

"And I said, 'Yes, and what happened?'

" 'Well, the preacher on Sunday, after church, he gave us a lot of handbills . . . [and] if what those handbills say is true, we don't see how you can be supporting this fellow Smith.'

"I said, 'Why not?' "

The man from Shiloh Valley showed Roosevelt the handbill, which said that since the Roman Catholic Church only recognized Catholic marriages and baptism, if Smith became President, all Protestant marriages would become adulterous relationships and all children born to them would become illegitimate.

"I said, 'I think I am legally married to my wife even if Smith has been governor of New York for eight years. . . . Let's look at the other one. . . . I have got five pretty husky kids and I have every reason to believe they are legitimate." Smith lost several southern states, but did carry Georgia. In Meriwether County, the Catholic candidate also won.

The day when a farmer could sneak up to Roosevelt's shuttered bedroom window in the hours before dawn would soon come to an end. So would the day when he could drive his hand-controlled Ford around on educational trips for conversations with his neighbors. But for the three years after he began driving and before he was elected Governor, he had such freedom. Even after he was elected Governor, he found spare hours to pay such visits. A farmer with land to sell in the years 1929 to 1932 might not have been surprised to see the new Model A drive into his front yard, with Roosevelt at the wheel, tieless, collar open, shirt sleeves rolled above his elbows, unaccompanied by any police guards. Roosevelt would ask him about the land, perhaps haggle a bit. His main concern on such occasions, and there were several, was not to purchase land. He usually turned the details of that over to agents—a local lawyer or the manager of the farm he bought in 1927. His main concern was, as Mrs. Killian put it, to get to know his neighbors. He may not have got to know every white man in the county, but he got to know many of them, and he got to know every *type*, economically and socially speaking.

Until 1932, he seemed genuinely at ease with them, and they seemed genuinely at ease with him. He became a celebrity nationally and locally again in 1928, after winning the governorship, and that marked the beginning of the end of his totally relaxed relationship with those Meriwether Countians he knew only casually. His interlude as a private person who was allowed the privileges of privacy was over. One thousand Georgians were at the train station in Warm Springs the night he came there two days after that election. No such welcome had ever been seen at any visit or homecoming there before. The town's population was under 1,000; the county's was 22,000. Though he met a few more Georgians he had not met before (local political leaders, including Sheriff J. B. Jarrell, gave a party for him), he noticed that his celebrity and his security needs began to intrude. Model A visits with bodyguards Gus Gennerich or Earl Miller along became the rule. The solo trips were exceptions. Otis Moore, who worked on Roosevelt's farm in that period (he would later manage it) recalled several occasions when Roosevelt did drive up alone and explained, "I slipped away from 'em, Oat."

After Roosevelt became President, the problem of casual face-to-face visits with neighbors became almost—but not quite—impossible. Gus and Earl now had Marines and Secret Service details to help keep an eye on Roosevelt. They were supposed to at all times. Public curiosity about the President was enormous. The extent of that curiosity suggests by contrast how accepted rich man Roosevelt and even Governor Roosevelt had become.

Roosevelt's first visit to Warm Springs as President was for Thanksgiving, 1933. He arrived on a Friday to another impressive public welcome. He drove to his new cottage, the Little White House. All day that Sunday sightseers drove up the clay road leading to it. They were not allowed to come all the way. Some sightseers even flew over in chartered planes, a real rarity in 1933.

On Monday, Roosevelt, his mother, Missy LeHand and Gus Gennerich got into his hand-controlled car and drove into town. He expected to be treated as usual by his old friends and acquaintances. It was a pretty warm day. He drove to the drugstore and honked his horn. The *Warm Springs Mirror* depicted what happened as a routine little transaction no different from similar Rooseveltian visits of the past: "When President Roosevelt stopped at a drugstore in town for a soda this week he shook hands and chatted with the oldest resident of Warm Springs, Judge A. C. Dunn.

"The President inquired after the health of Judge Dunn, who is 88 years old, and told the Justice of the Peace, who has known the President since Mr. Roosevelt first came to Warm Springs, that he was looking splendidly."

Judge Dunn seems to have been somewhat relaxed, but other Warm Springs residents must not have been. The *New York Times* reported that after Roosevelt's "casually ordered soda water for three," villagers began to gather around his car. A boy brought the three glasses of refreshment, then stood back with the rest of the crowd and stared as the drinks were consumed. "In the midst of the curious silence, the President hastily gulped his drink, started his car and hurried back to the Warm Springs Foundation, where the patients and staff have not registered such embarrassing awe in his presence." He went for a drive about the countryside that afternoon with his Secretary of the Interior, Harold Ickes, but did not stop for any more small talk or visits.

The novelty did wear off somewhat. A Secret Service

agent has described a later presidential visit to Warm Springs. The President drove about the county for an hour on a bright Sunday afternoon. He was in his Ford with the top down, accompanied by Agent Tommy Qualters and a White House secretary. Agents followed in another car. Suddenly the President decided to go into town for "an ice cream soda. . . . This created some concern to the detail [the agent wrote] as we had no prior notice of a stopover and consequently, there was no time to make our usual pre-visit security check.

"There were two old-timers sitting on the steps of the drugstore in the sun; they were playing checkers on an old checker board using bottle caps for checker men." The President stopped his car just in front of them and flashed a big smile. One said, "Howdy." Neither doffed his cap or otherwise indicated any deference. They continued the game. One got up at one point, walked over to the curb and spit some tobacco in the gutter. The agents from the second car had formed a loose guard around the President's car "to intercept anyone who might attempt to approach the President's car," but the checker player did not seem threatening. When Qualters, a genial Boston Irishman, told the men, pointing, that one of the President's guards was a local boy, the reply was a laconic, "He don't look like he's got much muscle to me." Roosevelt threw back his head and howled, and off the little caravan drove.

The Secret Service's responsibilities were part of the reason Roosevelt's freedom of motion was restricted on his visits to Georgia. But once in a while he would get away from them for a few minutes. That only happened in two places, Hyde Park and Warm Springs. Usually, it was just a game to Roosevelt. He liked to tease the agents. Once at

Warm Springs after a workout in the pool, he stayed on for a few minutes of play. Soon he was the only person in the water. Physiotherapist Alice Plastridge was on the edge of the pool. One agent stood several feet away. Others were just beyond the pool area. There were three pools at the time, with covered canal-type connecting links between them. Roosevelt noticed the nearby agent was looking the other way and said to Plastridge, "Watch this." He ducked underwater, swam through to one of the other pools and hid under some steps. The suddenly empty pool touched off a mad scramble of agents, first alarmed, then embarrassed. Roosevelt's guffaw could be heard in the dressing rooms many yards away, said Plastridge.

There were rare occasions when Roosevelt's forays about the countryside at Warm Springs (and Hyde Park) that were not frolicsome caused problems for the Secret Service detail. He liked to investigate the woodlands in Georgia and New York. Some trails would allow his little Model A or, later, his hand-controlled Plymouth convertible, access, but were impossible for the longer, wider and heavier vehicles the agents usually rode in. Such escapes were always about as short-lived as the swimming-pools incident.

Restrictions on his privacy and his ability to discuss life's realities with plain people face to face must have been especially galling to Roosevelt. He had always been a man who liked to see for himself. When he became crippled and could no longer go to many of the places he would have liked to, he enlisted Eleanor, taught her what to look for, what questions to ask, in prison kitchens, coal mines—everywhere. But even with his crippling illness, Roosevelt could still go in his succession of autos with their ingenious controls. One biographer contends that he learned the technique of explaining complicated national and international problems in simple, conversational terms through meetings with his rural neighbors. This biographer also says the visits were even more important in that they made "people problems" of the problems of a depressed nation. "Roosevelt [came] to know and appreciate the thinking of a number of quite ordinary people. . . . The plain people of the South were not an abstraction to Roosevelt; he regarded them as his friends and neighbors." That seems not to have been generally understood at the time of his ascendancy. "[Roosevelt] is a patron of politics," the *New Republic* said in 1932. "He, like Woodrow Wilson, condescends toward the people he would help and the problems he would solve. It is true, he makes excellent speeches about the 'forgotten man,' but he is no spokesman for that man by any blood brotherhood; he has just read about him in books."

The theme of a radio address Roosevelt gave from Albany a few weeks before that issue of the *New Republic* appeared was "the forgotten man at the bottom of the economic pyramid," and in fact, it was people he *knew* he was talking about. He attacked Republicans as "shallow thinkers" who did not realize that "approximately one-half of our whole population, fifty or sixty million people, earn their living by farming or in small towns whose whole existence immediately depends on farms. They have today lost their purchasing power. Why? They are receiving for farm products less than the cost to them of growing these farm products. The result of this loss of purchasing power is that millions of people engaged in industry in the cities cannot sell industrial products to the farming half of the nation. This brings home to the city worker that his own employment is directly tied up with the farmer's dollar. . . . I cannot escape the conclusion that one of the essential parts of a national program of restoration must be to restore purchasing power to the farming half of the country. . . .

"Closely associated with this first objective is the problem of keeping the home-owner and the farm-owner where he is, without being dispossessed through the foreclosure of his mortgage. His relationship to the great banks of Chicago and New York. . . . His is a relationship to his little local bank or local loan company. It is a sad fact that even though the local lender does not want to evict the farmer or home-owner by foreclosure procedures, he is forced to do so in order to keep his bank or company solvent. . . ."

Roosevelt was talking about people who were his neighbors and, in some cases, his friends in Warm Springs. James Farley once wrote that Roosevelt was a snob. But from his youth he seems to have been clearly committed to democratic principles, first in the theoretical sense, as he moved in circles composed only of people like himself, in Hyde Park, Groton, Harvard, Columbia and the first years in the Wall Street law firm of Carter, Ledyard and Milburn. Gradually, through Democratic party politics, then through his years in Georgia, he came to be democratic in every sense. As a college student, Roosevelt wrote that the Roosevelts were more virile than other Dutch families in the Hudson River Valley because they had "the democratic spirit . . . instilled in them at birth." He meant by the phrase "democratic spirit" a sort of noblesse oblige. Aristocrats had a duty to assist all. But by 1932 Roosevelt had come to believe as well in that democratic spirit that meant answers to problems and values of worth could be found among all sorts of individuals and classes.

Radio journalist Stanley High had a better reading than

Farley. "Roosevelt, in his personal relationships, is whole-heartedly a democrat," he said. "Snooty people are as much on his black list as prima donnas." Roosevelt wrote a marvelously revealing letter home from one of the cruises of the *Larooco*. He had gone ashore at Palm Beach, but quickly fled back to the ship, bored with the wealthy socialites there.

It was not just Roosevelt's Meriwether County rural neighbors who had been suffering the economic losses the pre-Depression years brought to the South. Roosevelt, himself, became one of them in fact as well as spirit, and his "Roosevelt Farms" was about as hard hit as were those of his neighbors.

## A note on sources for this chapter

Previously mentioned sources were again helpful, as was *Hi-Ya, Neighbor* by Ruth Stevens and *F.D.R. Columnist*, Donald Scott Carmichael (editor). The checkers incident is described in a letter to the author from Henry Thomas. Reverend Harry reconstructed the Roosevelt-sharecropper conversation. The use of dialect may mislead some readers. The unpublished Harry manuscript suggests that he was far ahead of his time and place in extending dignity as well as charity to blacks. The biographer referred to is Frank Freidel, whose multivolume work on Roosevelt was the beginning of research not only for this chapter, but for this book. He is also author of the invaluable *F.D.R. and the South*.

# *Not a Gentleman Farmer*

Franklin Roosevelt had always been a farmer in his heart. His father had cattle and timber on his Hyde Park land. He took the boy on inspection tours. Franklin joined the Grange as a young adult, after he had begun practicing law in Manhattan. When he served briefly in the New York State Legislature before becoming Assistant Secretary of the Navy, he specialized in agricultural and conservation matters. And when he was Governor he gave high priority to farm matters. For instance, he set up an Agriculture Advisory Committee which reduced taxes on farms and increased spending for education in rural areas. He liked to boast about his knowledge of farm problems, even before he had firsthand knowledge of them, and he liked to tease his city friends about the growing gap between city and rural life-styles. "Look, Grace," he said to his secretary Grace Tully once on a trip, pointing out the train window. "That's a cow."

At least as early as 1926, or within about a year and a half after his first visit to Warm Springs, Roosevelt began buying farmland and woodland there. He bought some land from the Harts, the Columbus people whose cottage he occupied on his first trips to Warm Springs, and bits and pieces of other holdings. Land was cheap in Georgia in the mid-1920s. According to Roosevelt's ledgers, he bought one 100-acre parcel on the side of Pine Mountain for $350. This was worthless by the normal standards of the day, but it was adjacent to a favorite spot of his, Dowdell's Knob, which offered a breathtaking view of Shiloh Valley—the Shenandoah Valley of the South, locals termed it. He got a road built to the Knob.

Farmland was cheap, too. There is some confusion in records and memories about the exact details of his acquiring the centerpiece of what came to be known as Roosevelt Farms. That was the Pine Mountain farm owned and run, when Roosevelt first arrived, by E. B. Doyle. Doyle apparently got into debt and sold his farm to Roosevelt after some earlier arrangement between the two didn't work out. Roosevelt's acquaintance with Doyle was another of those involvements that gave him a good close-up look at what economic depression could do to its victims. The Doyles were educated people from a middle-class background. Mrs. Doyle's father had been a small-town merchant. He was ruined when the boll weevil ruined his farmer customers. Ed Doyle's troubles were caused by, or at least complicated by, a small-town bank's failure, also induced by crop failures.

However the details were worked out between the two, Roosevelt's ledger shows that as of December 31, 1927, his assets included the "Hart farm" of unspecified acreage and the "Doyle farm" of 310½ acres. He valued the former at

$4,074.33 and the latter at $5,075. He added a couple of other parcels in 1927, one of approximately 50 acres and the other of approximately 60 acres. Each cost about $50 an acre. He added to this again and again. Soon his total acreage was over 1,100 acres in Meriwether County and 1,600 in adjoining Harris County. In both counties, the overwhelming majority of the land was in woodland or forest range. Probably never more than 300 acres were actually cultivated. Almost all of that was in the Meriwether County part of the farm, near the foundation and the cottages. The farmhouse and barn were also in Meriwether.

Doyle ran the farm for Roosevelt as resident manager, living on in the house there. It was actually a tenant's house that Doyle had taken over when his own burned down. Later he moved into town to make it easier for his children to go to school.

Meriwether County was a cotton-and-peaches agriculture center. Those two crops were mainstays of Georgia's economy. But for Meriwether's some 1,500 farmers in the middle 1920s, as for all Georgia cotton growers, cotton was risky business. The average Georgia cotton farmer lost money from 1925 through 1930—and things got worse after 1930. As for peaches, their return on investment and labor had dwindled to the point that when one Meriwether farmer had enough and pulled up half his orchard, Doyle wrote Roosevelt that what they ought to do was uproot all of theirs. Eventually (but after Doyle left) there was no orchard of commercial size. This was in a county that led "the Peach State" in peach production through the mid-1930s.

It was cotton that Roosevelt wanted most to get away from in Georgia. He believed that the state's endemic poverty would never be solved as long as so many of its farmers —owners, tenants and sharecroppers—looked to King Cotton. In 1920, 20 percent of all Georgia's farmland was devoted to cotton.

Later, when he got to be President, Roosevelt supported programs that would force farmers to limit severely the amount of cotton planted. But before that, and during his presidency, he also sought to demonstrate to Georgia farmers that there were better ways to farm, and that a good living could be made from other practices. He was interested in timber as a cash crop, in poultry, in grapes, in goats, in a variety of vegetables, in everything. He was especially interested in cattle. The whole point of his ownership of a Georgia farm was to demonstrate to other farmers that a farm could be profitable. He was not one of those "gentleman farmers" picking up cheap farmland and hiring cheap labor, in Georgia as elsewhere, to enjoy a leisurely part-time life "on the land."

In fact, the first adviser Roosevelt talked to about his plan told him bluntly that he would not help him if such was his desire. "Not only would such a 'demonstration' be useless, it might be worse than that," W. Tapley Bennett told him. "It would be harmful."

Bennett had been an "agriculturist" with the Central of Georgia Railroad from 1921 to 1926. Like Roosevelt, the railroad wanted to see a diversified agriculture in the South. Bennett's duties included giving away purebred bulls and cows as prizes in 4-H shows. In 1926 he went to work as county agent in Spalding County, adjacent to Meriwether. His reputation as an aggressive and innovative student of farm matters reached Roosevelt through mutual political friends. He had Missy LeHand call Bennett over to Warm Springs for a talk. The talk took place in Roosevelt's new cottage in 1926. The two men conversed while a barber from the village cut Roosevelt's hair.

"I want to farm just like the local farms do. The only difference is, I want to make a profit," Roosevelt said.

"Good," said Bennett. "Gentlemen farmers make it appear that even rich men can't make money farming, so why should anyone else try?" Roosevelt kept saying he wanted to concentrate on cattle. Bennett kept warning him against that gentleman-farmer approach. When Roosevelt said that he didn't want to do *any*thing that his neighbors couldn't do, they had a real meeting of the minds. Bennett got Roosevelt to agree to breed local scrub cattle with a registered Shorthorn bull and build the stock up that way. Roosevelt said he would even let his neighbors use his registered bull free to improve their own stock. One thing that stuck in Bennett's mind ever after, and which convinced him that Roosevelt was a real cattleman who meant business, was that Roosevelt could recall the names and registration numbers of his father's herds of long ago. "I was stunned," Bennett said, "then over-elated!"

Bennett left the meeting and bought Roosevelt 30 native cows for $16 a head. He bought a Shorthorn bull in Belvedere, Tennessee, for $150. A famous experiment was about to get under way.

Roosevelt was by no means the first Georgia farmer to try to make money with cattle or other stock. Bennett had given away some 350 registered bulls and cows for the Central of Georgia. A few other wealthy farm owners were trying to make cattle pay. Not only cattle. Ralph G. Wright of Buffalo, New York, bought a farm near Roosevelt's in the late 1920s and began raising sheep. Ed Doyle worked there part-time while managing Roosevelt's farm. Roosevelt's friend Cason Callaway made his fortune in the family textile business, then turned to an attempt to revolutionize agriculture in his native state with a variety of new crops, products and practices. And there were others. But what made Roosevelt's farm, and particularly his cattle, significant was that he became so famous. His Georgia farm reaped a bonanza of publicity. His ideas therefore received a much wider audience than Bennett—or anyone else— could have otherwise won for those ideas in so short a period of time.

Before he became President—before he became Governor—Roosevelt was a much-invited speaker at civic and community organizations around the state. He often spoke on agricultural matters. He was effective. A La Grange, Georgia, farmer, Joe L. Young, recalled years later going to a meeting where Roosevelt and Charles Herty spoke. Herty told about his new procedures for making pulpwood out of the pine that grew abundantly in south Georgia and had been considered only of limited use. Then Roosevelt told stories about huge, beautiful, profitable European forests he had seen, and predicted that they could be duplicated in Georgia. Young and his father went out and immediately began planting pine seedlings. That they did it at all would have made Roosevelt proud. That they did in an abandoned cotton patch would have thrilled him.

Young later became a successful cattleman, himself. He liked to reminisce about just what agricultural reformers like Roosevelt, Bennett, Callaway and the others were up against. Poor Georgia farmers were suspicious of new ideas, afraid of new departures, especially those that involved new responsibilities. At one meeting near Warm Springs around 1930, the idea of poultry raised on a large enough scale to produce income was discussed. When the question of what to feed the chickens came up, a surprised old farmer exclaimed, "Feed 'em? Feed 'em? Hell, if I have to feed 'em, I don't want 'em!" He expected the chickens to scratch for themselves, as did the few birds that many farmers kept running around their barnyards.

Roosevelt's herd increased in the years before he became President. The herd quickly reached about 150 head. Other farmers were watching his lead, and many were following it. Roosevelt let Doyle improve the herd somewhat as it grew. He let him buy 13 Black Angus in 1930. But he did not go the gentleman-farmer route. He did not get out too far ahead of his neighbors. When in 1932 Henry Wallace came down to Warm Springs, he thought the Roosevelt cattle were of poor quality. But later, as he traveled around the Southeast as Secretary of Agriculture, he realized they were typical.

In the late 1920s and first few years of the 1930s, Roosevelt kept after Doyle to turn cotton land over to pasturage. Though Doyle was an experienced farmer who knew Georgia weather and flora more intimately than Roosevelt did, as often as not it was Roosevelt advising Doyle rather than vice versa on farm operations. It was almost a partnership. On October 6, 1930, in the midst of his reelection campaign, Roosevelt wrote Doyle replying to a suggestion about trading some scrub cattle for some Herefords. "How about putting in a little black medic in the old pasture at the right time? It may not be winter-killed if you put it in soon, broad cutting it very lightly."

The Roosevelt example had its impact. At least in one sense, this occurred faster than Roosevelt expected. In 1929 he wrote Doyle to buy 15 breeding cows. He told him to pay $15 per head, about what Bennett had paid two years before. Doyle found the cows averaged over $25 each. There were many factors behind that price rise, of course, Roosevelt's example and celebrity being among them.

His celebrity after he was elected President far exceeded

what it had been. That was true in Georgia as elsewhere. After an incident at the Southeastern World's Fair, his cattle operation was even more celebrated. The fair, held in Atlanta every fall, was a typical "state fair" event, with amusements, rides, sideshows and agricultural exhibits.

Tap Bennett either misled or was misquoted by a reporter for the *Atlanta Constitution*. Bennett was superintendent of the stock department of the fair for 1933. The story that resulted from the mixed-up interview was to the effect that "Roosevelt cattle" would be on display at the fair. Bennett told the fair's director, Mike Benton, a flamboyant showman, that he couldn't do that. All the President had in the way of cattle were halfbreeds raised on his farm, which weren't appropriate for the fair, plus their calves, plus registered sires bought elsewhere—which weren't technically "Roosevelt cattle."

After a heated discussion about what was beginning to look like an embarrassment, Bennett got permission from Benton to order some top-grade ready-for-market steers from Chicago. While they were en route to Atlanta, Bennett went to Warm Springs and got some of Roosevelt's halfbreeds, a Hereford sire, plus several calves. He set up a red-white-and-blue bunting-decorated exhibit in which the sire was in one pen, then the halfbreeds, then the three-quarter-breed calves, then the handsome beef cows from Chicago. According to a news story after the fair opened, the exhibit was the hit of the show. "New Deal Calves from Roosevelt Farms at Warm Springs Show Way to Farmer," the headline writer for the *Constitution* wrote over a story and picture of four of the white-faced three-quarter-breeds.

Bennett gave up his other duties to stay with the exhibit. His spiel to the thousands who flocked to the exhibit was quoted thusly in the newspaper:

"These folks are looking at a plan—a demonstration of action. They are being convinced visually that President Roosevelt is a man of action. Other Georgia farmers have talked of plans for stabilizing the livestock industry in the state, but this farmer, President Roosevelt, put that plan into a fact and the result is here."

There was a sign over the pens: "The practical and economical method of establishing a beef cattle industry is to start with native cows and one registered bull. Improve the pastures and grazing. Grow more feed."

Bennett would tell crowds that the arrangement told a story. "With these [pointing to Herefords] and these [pointing to halfbreeds], we get these little critters, that develop into those that you see in that pen [pointing to the stockyard's prize animals]. That last pen of beef cattle ready for market represents the objective of every Georgia stock grower. . . ."

Bennett probably never said the cattle in the last pen were *actually* bred on Roosevelt's farm. But he probably never said they weren't, either. The exhibit remained popular throughout the fair's season of ten days or so. So popular was it, in fact, that Bennett found himself on duty from 7 A.M. to 1:30 A.M. every day, answering questions and giving his speech.

The *Constitution*'s final publicity bonus was an interview with a farmer from Pike County, Georgia, who said he had decided on the spot to buy a Hereford bull. "There will be a few less acres of cotton, more alfalfa and pea-vine hay and one more registered Hereford bull in Pike County at this time next year," the paper said.

President Roosevelt apparently did not hear the story until the next month, when he came to Warm Springs for Thanksgiving. He sat listening to Bennett tell it in all its detail. When the story was over, he looked at Bennett for a moment, then guffawed, throwing his head back "just like his neck was on hinges," in Bennett's phrase. "It just went all the way back."

The "Roosevelt cattle" exhibit produced a bonus. Paid attendance to the livestock exhibit far exceeded expectations. Moreover $35,000 of it was invested in Coca-Cola stock, and, according to Bennett, the growth in value of that stock over the next few years kept the fair afloat.

That same October, the U.S. Department of Agriculture enrolled Roosevelt (No. 18,126) as a breeder of registered cattle. "Purebred Sires Exclusively Used on This Farm," a sign there proclaimed to the world. But behind the sign, the profit situation was not as rosy as it had been at the fair.

Despite his desire to make his farming operation profitable, Roosevelt soon found that that was easier said than done. The "Southern Depression" before 1929 was bad; the national Depression following the crash of that year made things worse even in Georgia. In the year before the crash, per capita farm income in Georgia had been only $145. By the year Roosevelt was elected President, that had dropped to $74.

On his own farm, Roosevelt found he was playing the gentleman farmer—if not the squire or the patron—in the sense that he was subsidizing his work force. They were hard workers; they were proficient; Roosevelt's overseership was informed and enlightened—and all of this did not add up to earnings in excess of expenses and investment.

In part this was due to Roosevelt's being too enlightened. Having a full-time farm manager, to whom he paid $100 a month and provided a house, was unusual, even extravagant for those times in that place. No cotton farm in Meriwether County had a manager at that time. The largest peach orchards did have managers, but none received that sort of pay. In addition to paying Doyle, Roosevelt also paid $50 a month to Otis Moore to handle the cattle herd. That was about what the managers made at the best peach orchards. Roosevelt's payroll was almost surely the highest of any farm of similar size in southwest Georgia. In March 1930, for example, his monthly payroll was $195—$100 for Doyle, $50 for Moore, $15 for one "wage hand" and $10 each to three others. At that rate, he could expect his annual payroll to be $2,340. Yet when he prepared his 1929 income tax return that month, he had to notice that his gross income on the farm the year before had been only $2,275.35. And of course, there were a great many more expenses than just payroll—seed, fertilizer, fencing, building repairs, equipment maintenance, etc. As the Depression deepened, Roosevelt increased his payroll. Moore got $75 a month after January 1931; and the wage hands got raises to $25 for one and $17.50 each for two others. (One was let go.)

In fact, in 1929, his expenses exceeded gross income by a whopping $3,184.08. At that point the farm was still essentially a cotton farm, with about two-thirds of its income derived from cotton, a situation Roosevelt eventually ended —temporarily. Income from cattle in 1929 was only $65.41. The farm was gradually going out of the peach business. Doyle and Roosevelt had been urging such a course on each other from the start. "My labor bill for picking, packing, grading peaches added to the cost of containers amounts to more than all the peaches will bring," Doyle wrote Roosevelt the summer before he decided to run for Governor. Roosevelt wrote on several occasions in the next few years that he saw no future for the peach business.

Roosevelt urged other enterprises. For example, he had what was apparently the first Concord grape orchard in the area. It had never done well in south Georgia. Two men named Scott and Stuckey were trying to develop a better-yielding grape to substitute for the native scuppernong. Roosevelt knew of their work and ordered a vineyard on a slope of his own farm. In early years this varied from 2 to 10 or 12 acres. It brought in little income at first, $22.15 in 1929, for example. But later, after Roosevelt became so well known, roadside stand sales and sales to an Atlanta winery amounted to over $2,000 worth of grapes one year.

Roosevelt also raised, for sale at a roadside stand, peaches, spinach, peppers, watermelons, cantaloupes, eggplants, tomatoes, string beans and a number of other vegetables, and there was mohair from Angora goats, wool from sheep. Roosevelt wrote Doyle in 1929 that what he ought to do is get neighboring farmers to bring their produce to his stand for him, Doyle, to sell. "If we can make even a slight profit, it keeps the trade going," he said.

The grapes never caught on with other farmers in the area, but Roosevelt and his friend Cason Callaway did get local farmers to try apple orchards. This worked out well enough for Roosevelt to boast to a group of agriculture writers years later when he was President that "for the first time" local apples could be bought in grocery stores in south Georgia. "That is not very encouraging news for the people of the state of Washington, but it is a wholly correct development," he said.

In 1930 the farm suffered further losses, of about the same size as in 1929. In May 1931, Doyle became so discouraged he wrote to Roosevelt suggesting a change of directions. "First, I want to advise you in a general way of conditions on the farms. We have a large acreage planted to corn for cattle and mule feed and it's all up and growing off nicely. Our grape vines are extra fine. We pruned them correctly and fertilized them well and will, I am sure, have a fine crop of nice grapes. . . . I let Mack Copeland [a black hired hand] have a farm of thirty acres with the understanding that he could pay his rent by working an additional thirty acres in the feed stuffs for us. That saves our having to furnish Mack any fertilizer, supplies, etc., and I believe we will come out better than we would by letting him work cotton and corn on shares, for the thirty acres of cattle feed will be fully as valuable as our half of his cotton & corn crops would be and will certainly be more useful to us."

He said the peach trees were heavily laden, but doubted if they would be profitable. "That brings us to the cattle. Prices are still as bad as they could be it seems. They haven't gone up although they have been some lower than at present. We had a pretty tough time of it carrying so many through the winter . . . but it certainly looked last Fall like it would be the wise thing to hold on to them, but prices and conditions got worse instead of better. We lost several head of scrub calves and three grown scrub cows during the winter, which we hated very much, but it could have been much worse. So now, we are starting another Spring with 150 head, scrub and pure bred, and the pastures are getting in fine shape, and in the meantime all the cattle are putting on flesh and looking better every week. We have fifty head steers and cows that we want to put on the market within the next six weeks, and even if prices do not get any better I am inclined to go ahead and sell them, if agreeable with you, for when they get good fat they should be put on the market, I believe. Then later on in the year we plan to sell off all the balance except the pure bred beef type and what calves we have on hand at that time. . . .

"I still believe there is money to be made in cattle, providing a fellow hangs on until conditions get better," Doyle wrote, but added he was sure Roosevelt must be getting discouraged about the continuing loss of money on the farm, "and this leads me to make a few suggestions or recommendations to you.

"The first is, you might have me as fast as I can, close out the business and call it quits. . . . " He said he didn't think that was a good idea, now that so much had been invested in cattle and pastures.

"The second suggestion would be that I can let Mr. Moore go, and try to handle the whole situation myself. . . ." But he said he was not physically able to plow, as Moore was, so he didn't think that was a good idea.

A third suggestion was to get Moore to operate "the entire project" on a fifty-fifty basis, with Roosevelt providing nothing but half the cost of each year's fertilizer. "This would eliminate your having to spend money each month for that abominable payroll. . . ."

A fourth suggestion was to sell all the scrub cattle, keeping the 36 head of purebred then on the farm, add "about seventy head beef type in grown cows, either bred or ready to breed, so we could start right in raising calves." Doyle estimated the cost of this change in the herd plus a new barn and feed mill would cost "a few thousand dollars . . . [but] we would then have a herd you could feel proud of. . . ." He foresaw making an annual profit on such an arrangement of $2,000.

"And should you think it best to accept either the first or the third recommendation, I want to request of you to please help me get something to do in the North, 'New York City or anyplace.' I realize there is not much here for a man to get into and I realize also that there are better opportunities in the North for a man who will try. . . ."

Since it is the contention of this book that Franklin

Roosevelt learned a great deal about the nation's economic realities and the morale of its people in such sources, the letter is quoted at length. The last two sentences are worth a chapter of their own, and the next chapter is that.

To abandon his cattle operation for a relatively expensive purebred herd would have been an admission of failure, reducing Roosevelt Farms to the gentleman-farmer status. To have gotten rid of a manager and turned the farm over to a tenant who might or might not be able to make a go of it would have been worse than failure: It would have been surrender. To reduce the payroll by a few hundred dollars would have helped not at all, considering that losses each year were in the thousands.

What Roosevelt did was to continue as before. Losses in 1931 were again just over $3,000. Same thing in 1932. When he became President, Roosevelt named Doyle U.S. Marshall. Doyle's family teased him that Roosevelt only did it to stop the losses on the farm. But of course, they and he knew the problem there was not one man's fault. Otis Moore became manager. Losses continued, apparently for the rest of Roosevelt's life. His income tax returns show that he lost over $2,000 in 1933, over $3,500 in 1935, over $1,700 in 1936. Other tax returns were not available when research was done on this book, but other evidence suggests the losses continued. For instance, in 1938 Moore wrote Roosevelt that he wanted to put wage hands on shares. He said it would save some money.

In 1936 Moore had written Roosevelt that another way to make money was—to go back to cotton. Roosevelt had weaned his Georgia operation off that, but when Moore asked plaintively if he couldn't put in 50 acres—"it would mean so much to the farm"—Roosevelt replied, ". . . I have no objections to your putting in forty or fifty acres this spring, providing you get the O.K. of the Committee on this use of the land." Under New Deal agricultural policies, cotton production was limited. Farmers had to have permission to plant it. When FDR stopped planting it, the policy called for federal payments for taking the land out of production. He refused to let Moore accept such payments, for the obvious reasons that he was not retiring land for the reason the other farmers were—and because he knew it would be used against him as a political issue. In fact, he was charged with it anyway. Roosevelt liked the following "farmer story" because it made a point about cotton's futility *and* about his critics' ignorance. "Down in Georgia," he told a farm group in 1935, in a discussion of New Deal policies, "an editor of a great metropolitan paper was visiting me down there in the summertime when I showed him my farm with 40 or 50 acres of cotton when the cotton was nearly grown but before the bolls had formed. Looking out over the cotton fields, he said to me, 'What a large number of raspberries they grow down here!' Well, raspberries was right, because at four and a half cents a pound for cotton his mistake was, perhaps, a natural one." FDR thought cotton was a doomed crop in Georgia. He liked to quote Cason Callaway: "You could grow anything in Georgia except corn and cotton, and yet those are the two things that the state grows." Roosevelt's 1936 crop failed.

Quoting Callaway to that effect at a press conference, Roosevelt went on to say that synthetic textiles were being developed that would replace cotton as a material for clothing. He said he hoped that eventually even Georgia pine could be used as a source for such synthetic materials. Making pine a profitable substitute for cotton as a textile source was believing in an old dream with a vengeance. For Roosevelt had long believed that timber could do much for the

South. Though he turned down some early requests to cut his trees for commercial uses, he believed in timbering as an industry. He thought trees as a cash crop offered salvation to impoverished Georgia farmers, somewhat like cattle did, so he had Doyle blanketing his mountain in pine seedlings from very early on. In 1929 alone he put in 5,600 pines. But personally, Roosevelt put forest conservation (and creation) ahead of tree farming.

Otis Moore may have been hired as a cattle foreman originally, but he was a sawmill man at heart. Moore's habits with cattle were sometimes unorthodox. He let the cattle graze in the peach and apple orchards. This infuriated Bennett. Once at a press conference in Warm Springs, after he became President, Roosevelt replied to a question about this practice by saying that his cattle "can live up there [on the mountaintop orchard land] but I cannot fatten them, and as long as I do not, I cannot get a decent price." Rex Tugwell was sitting in on the conference. He asked why the President didn't let them "get their growth up there and then bring them down and fatten them?" Roosevelt said that would work if he revamped the farm arrangement. Apparently some such revamping was done and the cattle spent more time in pasture thereafter.

Occasionally, Roosevelt's cattle were an embarrassment. In 1938 a Meriwether County farmer's wife wrote Roosevelt that the cattle had been "turned out . . . to make their living or die and I just say I have sure had a time with those cows. They have torn up all the shrubbery that I had. . . . Those cows almost drive us crazy." This in a neatly typed letter. There apparently was no reply. In 1940 another of his neighboring farmers wrote Roosevelt to complain that his cows had eaten some velvet beans on his farm. The letter was written on two sheets of 4 by 7 lined soft paper, the kind used in schools of the day. It was addressed "Mr. Franklin D. Roosevelt, Washington D.C." and began "Dear Sir . . . I am sorrow that I halft to write you about it. But Mr. Moore haven't paid me yet. And I need the money to buy some feed for my cow. . . . Yours very truly. . . ." Missy referred the letter to the Georgia Warm Springs Foundation, which paid the farmer $4.

Roosevelt relented on tree-cutting in 1935. He agreed to the cutting down of 200 "obviously mature" trees on the foundation's grounds to be sold to a federal agency then in the market for lumber. Otis Moore and some of his hands did the logging, and the sawing was done on the farm in partnership with a local lumber company. The 1935 enterprise worked out well. They sold over $700 worth of lumber. So Moore and his hands cut enough trees on Miss Georgia Wilkins's property adjoining Roosevelt's Little White House to earn $1,000 for the good lumber, then traded the scrap for a feed mill for the cattle. "Didn't have to pay out any cash at all," a proud Moore wrote the President. He had similar success in 1936 and 1937. He began pressing for permission to buy "a small outfit and operate it ourselves."

That finally came about in 1938. Right off the bat, the operation cost Roosevelt money, since the first sawing produced lumber there was no market for. The President had to advance Moore $500 to keep the crew together until conditions changed.

Otis Moore's place in the history of Roosevelt Farms is connected not only to the sawmill and cattle, but also to mules. After 1933, there were a number of stories in the press to the effect that Roosevelt owned the Georgia farm, but knew nothing about farming and left the decision making to hired men. Roosevelt and his White House aides allowed stories about the success and profitability of the farm to go unchallenged (except when asked directly, as for instance, when a Baltimore-published farm magazine inquired if the farm was truly a model in the profit-making sense; Roosevelt directed his press secretary to tell the editor that the farm did not make a profit, though he hoped some day it would). But they did not like the sort of stories that said Roosevelt was a phony farmer.

Moore read the stories and was troubled by them, too. He was also troubled by a visit from a reporter whose questions showed skepticism of Roosevelt's farming knowledge. So he suggested to Roosevelt that he—the President—*demonstrate* he was in control by purchasing two mules the farm needed. When the President came down for his Thanksgiving season vacation in 1934, a mule dealer brought a selection over to the farm. FDR, with the press corps and a few advisers in tow, drove over from the Little White House. A deal was made after the President displayed knowledge about mules.

Walter Trohan, the *Chicago Tribune* Washington correspondent, suggested the names for the new mules, Hop and Tug, after Roosevelt's advisers, Harry Hopkins and Rexford Tugwell, who were also there that day. The names stuck.

Good publicity resulted as expected. But in at least one case there was an unintentional result. A Lakewood, Ohio, man wrote this note after reading an Associated Press dispatch that described the trade-in pair as "old, wornout mules": "Mr. President—We very respectfully ask for information as to the ages and condition of these mules. . . . If the transaction is as thoughtless and heartless as the attached article indicates it is our opinion you should personally reconsider the case for the general good of both yourself and the animals. Respectfully, Don A. Cooper."

Two years later, the President got some additional flattering coverage of the event. This was prior to the presidential election and the story appeared in the influential *Breeder's Gazette*. The story dealt with the President's cattle, but it included this quote from Moore:

"Man . . . you should have been here for the mule trading about two years ago. I learned something myself that time. I thought I was a pretty good mule man, but Mr. Roosevelt showed me up. We had a pair of rather old mules that we decided should be traded for younger ones and the President concluded that he would do the trading himself. I was mighty glad when he decided that, for so many people had asked me [how much attention the President paid to the farm's operation]. I knew that after he finished the mule trade I would have a definite answer to that question at least. I had a mule dealer bring over about six mules one afternoon when the President could get off for a little while. Fortunately for myself, I thought, the President was delayed in getting here and I had almost an hour to look over the mules and decide which were the best and which were best suited for our type of farming here.

"You see . . . in our rather mountain type of farming here, heavy mules, over 1300 pounds, are not as well suited as under 1250. Well, I thought I had those fully docketed by the time the President drove up. The first shock I got was when we led out the mules we planned to trade. Now it had been almost a year since he had seen these two mules and I never thought he had paid much attention to them. But he called them by name as they came out of the barn and said to me, 'I rather hate to see old Lett go. She has made a mighty good mule.' Before I got over that, they started leading the other mules around. When they had led those mules around once, he had found two blemishes on them that I hadn't seen, and I had spent an hour going over them carefully. After that I was more than glad that he was doing the trading, and he sure made a good one. Don't you believe that he doesn't know every little thing that is going on and all about it. And he remembers every detail of it."

Hop and Tug became something of a joke for the press corps—a joke Roosevelt joined in. Here is an exchange from a press conference in the White House:

Q. Mr. President, there has been a screwworm epidemic in the Southeast.

A. What?

Q. A screwworm. Georgia is very much alarmed and it is also said that Warm Springs has been attacked. I wonder if they will get help from [a federal relief agency]?

A. What is it? . . . What does it affect?

Q. Animals—cows and horses.

Q. It works its way and spreads through the flesh. It is very bad.

A. My Lord! I hope it does not affect the two mules. (Laughter)

Q. It affects all warm-blooded animals. (Laughter)

A. Both sexes? (Laughter)

Q. You put creosote on it.

A. Well, we will have to get hold of Tug and Hop and go after it. . . .

Hop and Tug were not the only mules Roosevelt ever personally selected. He once bought a mule from banker and mule dealer Henry Kimbrough on a trial basis. When it worked out, he bought a second just like it. According to Tap Bennett, Roosevelt got the mules for about two-thirds their true value. "Kimbrough was willing to take a loss for the honor." A lot of people felt that way after Roosevelt became President, and though he had a general rule against accepting valuable gifts for the farm, he did accept some, including a pair of registered bulls from a Texan.

Over twenty years later, Tugwell interviewed Robert Copeland, son of a black wage hand on the Roosevelt farm and a worker there himself. No doubt to Tugwell's immense delight, the interview included this exchange:

TUGWELL: "How many mules did he usually have?"

COPELAND: ". . . Oh, Mr. Roosevelt bought two mules. I was with him. He bought two mules and he picked them himself and he named them. He named one Hopkins and the one Tugwell. Why Tugwell was the mule I plowed and Hopkins was the mule that my brother plowed."

TUGWELL: "You plowed Tugwell, did you?"

COPELAND: "Yes, sir. I plowed that mule, and that crazy mule ran away with me, coming down this hill right down here."

TUGWELL: ". . . I understand one of the mules was a good mule and the other one wasn't so good."

COPELAND: "That's right. Tugwell was the best mule and Hopkins he finally got to where he wasn't so good. They were both fine to start with though."

Roosevelt kept a close eye on his farm's operations not only before he went back into public office, but after. However, by the time Roy Durham succeeded Moore in 1940, he was preoccupied with the approaching war and two of his lieutenants seem to have done much of the overseeing. They were Tap Bennett, who was then managing a federal resettlement project nearby, and Louis Haughey, who was business manager at the Georgia Warm Springs Foundation. In a way which would certainly be frowned on in a later time, Roosevelt was quite casual about letting his roles as private citizen-farmer, President of the GWSF and Chief Executive of the nation intermingle. The foundation's tractor was often used to help the farm's mules (until the farm got its own in the late '30s); the farm provided lumber and foodstuffs to the foundation; Tap Bennett "moonlighted" as adviser to both farm and foundation while on the federal payroll. Roosevelt never had a second thought about using "Official Business-Government Notes" telegrams to send instructions to farm and foundation. No one questioned it then, and no harm was done. A strict cost-accounting study of these relationships would almost surely have shown that Roosevelt was a personal net loser on his conflicts of interests. He gave almost all of his Georgia land—about 2,600 acres—to the foundation.

If there was one aspect of his Georgia farm that meant more to him than the others, it was the trees. He had been a conservationist from youth. He had introduced some new concepts to south Georgia. Firebreaks cut on his woodlands as a protective measure were the first in the county. Different local people have taken credit for suggesting this to Roosevelt. At any rate, it was his example that prompted others to follow suit. In 1932 the Meriwether County Forestry Fire Prevention Association honored Roosevelt for his efforts in this field. He was presented the deed to the largest tree in the area, an oak with a 23-foot girth.

It was not just on his farm that Roosevelt nurtured and protected forests. The Georgia Warm Springs Foundation's grounds are a tree-lover's paradise. There are all sorts of trees, but pines dominate. In 1936 Henry Toombs, the architect at the foundation, wrote Roosevelt saying he thought oaks did better in forests than pines. As the pines die out on the foundation's campus, he suggested, they should be replaced by southern live oaks. Roosevelt wrote back that it was, after all, *Pine* Mountain, and Toombs got the point.

On another occasion, Roosevelt kept objecting to a Toombs proposal for a new building. The building as designed was a natural for the setting selected. But using that setting would have required cutting down some trees. Roosevelt said he favored changing the nature of the building, which led to the need for a new site, which saved the trees. Toombs said later he believed it was the site, not the nature of the building, that was the issue.

Roosevelt's interest in his Georgia trees seemed to increase as the years rolled on. At least it did not wane. In 1939 he met with a group of Georgia members of Congress at the Little White House. He told them he had spent the morning driving over his farmland looking at the pines he had had planted in 1929. He said the state of Georgia was going to plant some of its 33,000,000 pine seedlings on his and adjacent land, and he and a state forester were going to look for spots that afternoon. In 1941 he asked to be kept informed of the details of a tree-reforestation program, and O'Connor wrote him that some 50,000 trees would soon be planted.

Even in 1944, when he could not have been more preoccupied with the affairs of state, Roosevelt devoted time to his trees at Warm Springs. In January of that year, for one example, he "intercepted" a letter to Grace Tully from Fred Botts. Botts wanted to cut down a tree leaning near the Little White House. Roosevelt replied, "It is leaning away from the house and would not blow down on the house. . . . These trees have such a remarkable habit of not dying, [it] should not be removed until it dies." He also answered some letters from people he did not know about the trees and forests there that year.

Roosevelt's interest in his farm itself may not have remained as deep as his interest in his forests after a decade in the White House. But he certainly never became disinterested. When Tugwell interviewed Tap Bennett many years later, Tug expressed the opinion that Roosevelt lost interest in the farm after the war began. Tap nodded his head and said maybe, but even after the war started, when Roosevelt came to Warm Springs, "He always went straight to the farm."

## *A note on sources for this chapter*

Books not previously cited are *A Century of Georgia Agriculture* by Willard Range, *Political Animals* by Walter Trohan, *F.D.R., My Boss* by Grace Tully, and *In Search of Roosevelt* by Rexford G. Tugwell. The Toombs-Roosevelt correspondence and other papers of the architect that will be used extensively in a later chapter are in the Georgia State Archives. The clippings files of the *Atlanta Journal* and the *Atlanta Constitution* have been stripped of almost all pre-1945 items, but some useful material on Roosevelt's farm remains.

# Pine Mountain Valley

———————————◆———————————

Ed Doyle's willingness in 1931 to give up farming and seek a job in "New York City or anyplace" had to be a jolt to Roosevelt. He did not believe in a farm-to-city migration. All his life he had argued the rural environment was the better environment in every respect. "Country men and boys," he allowed a New York newspaper reporter to quote him as saying in 1911, make "better and more honest" politicians. When the rural economies failed, his idea was to salvage them or create new rural opportunities. While Roosevelt was Governor, there was a resettlement project at Cornell University that took submarginal farmland out of production and returned it to grassland and woods. The farmers were moved to nearby valleys where, with state aid, they would, theoretically at least, be able to create a more healthy economic environment. Roosevelt said at the time that he would like to see the national equivalent of that.

Roosevelt was familiar with the poverty of rural America—in Dutchess County and, painfully, in Meriwether

County. But he still believed the rural life was better than the urban life, particularly for those in bad economic straits. He not only opposed farm-to-city migration, he urged city-to-farm migration. In 1931 a New York City woman wrote him a desperate letter to the effect that all her husband's pay only paid the rent, leaving nothing for maintaining life. Governor Roosevelt replied that the family should consider moving to "a smaller community." He did more than exhort. In 1932 he announced plans for a program that would put out-of-work urban families on subsistence farms. The state would pay the rent and give the families tools, seed, etc. Roosevelt said this was an answer to the "relief problem," not the "farm problem."

Just as the experiment at Cornell offered one idea for a national program, so too did one that had been tried in Georgia about the same time. Roosevelt alluded to this early in 1934, explaining for the umpteenth time how much simpler it was, in his view, to deal with poverty in a rural rather than an urban setting. "Work for wages is not essential for [rural folk] as it is for city. The effort should be to make them self-sustaining. . . . The simplest illustration I know of is what we tried to do in Georgia a few years ago, the hog, home and cow campaign, where the government aided them to get the cow and let them pay for it over a period of years. In the long run, that is cheaper than buying milk for them." Of course, even families on subsistence farms need some money, he continued. A way to get money into their pockets is to insist that rural highway-building jobs be given to "the people who need it, again coming down to the essential element of need."

Roosevelt believed that highways for rural counties and increased electrification in those areas would bring industrial decentralization rather soon in states like New York, for subsistence farmers near their farms.

In the short run, nothing much came of these approaches; they certainly did not stop the movement of impoverished farmers to cities and large towns.

Nothing much dampened Roosevelt's own enthusiasm for country living, though. Thirty years after he told of seeing virtues in rural politicians that were not present in urban ones, he was telling reporters that country boys were healthier in certain respects and made better soldiers. This was at a press conference in October 1941. Asked about draft rejects, he said, "I would say offhand that on the heart disease thing, and the nervous disorders, you would find a higher percentage coming from the cities than you would from the farm. Now that's just a guess. But it is based on what you might call common sense reasoning. We farmers are not so nervous as you city slickers."

In the face of all commonsense reasoning, Roosevelt clung not only to the belief that rural life was always to be preferred, but also to the belief that the massive migrations of the 1930s and 1940s were just a passing phenomenon. There was a bloody race riot in Detroit in 1942. The President was asked to comment at a press conference. "This influx of population in Detroit is not a permanent thing," he said. ". . . And, well, about the only thing you can say on it is a word of advice to treat this as a temporary problem."

One of the most interesting efforts was Roosevelt's attempt to do on a national scale what had been tried on a small scale at Cornell while he was Governor. A Division of Subsistence Homesteads was set up in the Department of Interior in the first year of the New Deal, and it began planning such homesteads at various locations. The following year the Federal Emergency Relief Administration (FERA) brought a Texan, Lawrence Westbrook, to Washington to take over the planning of such homesteads. He believed that machines were *permanently* displacing workers, and that the answer to the problem was to create communities in which there were part-time jobs in cooperative agricultural and industrial enterprises, plus subsistence gardens for workers, plus recreational facilities. He and Dallas architect David Williams had had some success on a small scale in Texas. Williams, who went to Washington with Westbrook, was certainly a man after Roosevelt's heart. He believed that such communities could sprout everywhere. He proposed building 1,000,000 homes a year in rural communities, to be paid for with the savings from relief payments. The home building would create 2,000,000 jobs. Workers and plants would move from the cities. Town and farm would be united. Marginal land would be retired.

FERA began making loans and grants and offering guidance to rural clients. About 100 to 150 such communities were planned, but by 1935, with only 28 actually under way, a new unit of the new Works Project Administration, the Resettlement Administration, was given the responsibility for working with these communities. Of those 28, three were to be pilot projects; and after RA came in, only those three were kept going under the WPA's aegis. One of the three was in Arkansas, one was in Florida, and one was the Pine Mountain Valley community in Georgia, near Roosevelt's farm. Dowdell's Knob overlooked the valley.

Pine Mountain Valley was originally one of three such communities planned for Georgia. The Georgia corporation that ran it was chartered in October 1934. Roosevelt reviewed the Pine Mountain plans when they were submitted shortly thereafter, and Gay B. Shepperson, a social worker, the relief administrator in Georgia, was put in charge of the project. She was a protégé of the controversially liberal Aubrey Williams and a fiery New Dealer who alternately outraged and charmed politicians in the state with her outspokenness and willingness to meddle, even into patronage politics, usually the preserve of elected officials. She borrowed Tap Bennett to select and assemble the land for the project. Bennett was by then working for the federal agency implementing the new policy of sharply limiting cotton production. (Not the least reason there were tens of thousands of idle ex-farm workers in southern cities—and Detroit—was that cotton production was sharply reduced. Estimates of the number of tenant farmers and sharecroppers forced to leave farms because of the reductions reached as high as one million.)

Bennett selected 10,500 acres in the mostly barren but potentially productive valley. Several Negro families, trying to scratch out livings there, were either moved or their land was gerrymandered out of the project.

What Washington wanted at Pine Mountain was not so much *people* but "part of the necessary raw material for a beautiful plan," as Paul Conkin, the foremost student of Pine Mountain Valley, has put it. The colonists were thought of as types, not individuals. Washington specified able-bodied Georgians from large towns and cities who were between the ages of 25 and 50, were on relief because of vanished jobs, not incompetence, who had some education— and who were white. Not only were the colonists all white, they were all Protestants. Only a very few were from Harris County, in which the valley was located. They were from

Atlanta, Macon, Columbus, La Grange. Seventy percent had lived on farms at some time in their lives.

Amid a great surge of idealism and expectation, construction began on the houses, one- to three-bedroom models of native pine, each with a barn or shed. By the summer of 1935, the first colonists moved in, and they were busily tending to truck crops, orchards, dairy cattle, chickens and —cotton.

The community had a lot going for it, and if the idea could prevail anywhere, it should have been there. The President himself was personally committed to its success. The first manager of the community was a physician, who had a run-in with the planners over fees for local doctors. Roosevelt visited the aborning community late in 1935, signaling his interest in its success, while the dispute between planners and manager was going on. He suggested that Tap Bennett be brought back as manager to replace the doctor. Bennett didn't want to, but accepted a draft. His approach was less Utopian than the planners'. He believed the decision-making was a little too democratic and suspended it. This led some colonists, who were already upset because agricultural workers were making less money than construction workers, to protest in the most vigorous way, including burning down a barn. Bennett clamped down hard, called in the sheriff and had 26 families evicted. There were only 210 families living there at the time.

This seems not to have disturbed Roosevelt. Nor did charges that some of the directors of the new corporation set up to run Pine Mountain Valley were big businessmen at heart, running the cooperative ventures as corporations for profit. Nor did criticism to the effect that Pine

Mountain Valley had become "an old plantation without a landlord" bother him much. That was sort of what he hoped for. Criticism came from every quarter. Some conservatives said Pine Mountain Valley was nothing more than a Soviet collective.

Roosevelt went back to Pine Mountain Valley in March of 1937 for a very brief visit. The colonists gave him a flag. He was asked at a press conference in Warm Springs: "How do you think they're going to do?"

He replied: "All right." He said compared to the rest of the area, the homes and crops and businesses were "amazing."

Because Roosevelt's interest in Pine Mountain Valley was so much greater than in any other resettlement project —Paul Conkin called it "a unique relationship"—it was inevitable that some critics of it attacked it in terms of Roosevelt's role and in personal terms. They saw "clear paternalistic elements in his visits—the king of the realm, accompanied by local vassals or lords, visiting a prize manor and receiving the due obeisance and gratitude from the happy peasantry."

Well, the peasantry wasn't all that happy. After the barn-burning and evictions, there were always vacancies and a pretty consistent turnover. When jobs were available in the cities, colonists often quit the community for the city. It was not unusual to hear even those who preferred the rural life explain their stay at Pine Mountain Valley in terms of its being a good place to save money—with which they hoped someday to buy a farm of their own elsewhere. A permanent Utopia it was not for most.

Roosevelt visited Pine Mountain Valley again during his Thanksgiving season trip to Warm Springs in 1938. The show put on for his and his aides' benefit is perhaps what the lords-of-the-manor critics had in mind specifically. Roosevelt sat in his open car and listened to a 15-minute presentation of facts attesting to the success and happiness of the community: how many dozens of eggs produced, gallons of milk, number of cattle. He broke ground for the community's handsome new church, designed by Henry Toombs, Roosevelt's architect at Warm Springs (and at Hyde Park), to be built with lumber from Roosevelt's farm. The President sat for two hours in chilly fall weather observing a WPA-produced pageant with an orchestra and 550 participants, 400 of them in costume. "I hope you people realize that what you are doing here is not merely for yourselves, but, because of your example, there are lots and lots of people all over the country who are profiting by the example that you have set," he said.

As noted before, it was not really an example that any other community could hope to emulate. Whatever success it had was due to such special factors as the personal interest of the President of the United States.

Not that that is all that made it special. In Miss Shepperson and Tap Bennett, Pine Mountain Valley had two outstanding public servants. Some who have studied Pine Mountain Valley concluded that it never really operated the way liberals such as Westbrook and Williams wanted it to. This is based in part on the fact that Bennett was a conservative of sorts, and that Tugwell, the first chief of the Resettlement Administration, was openly opposed to the idea. Tugwell believed in redistributing land, but in 1933 he wrote, "I am inclined to believe that such settlements [as Pine Mountain Valley] will function merely as small eddies of retreat for exceptional persons; and that the greater part of our population will prefer to live and work in a more vigorous and active mainstream of a highly complex civilization."

But Tugwell was gone from this job by the beginning of 1937; and Will Alexander, the dean of southern liberals, was in charge. As for Tap Bennett's conservatism, it is good to remember how unconservative he had always been on agricultural matters. His was not a closed mind. More than that, however, he was the kind of public servant who saw his duty and did it. Here is Paul Conkin's tribute to Bennett: "[He] represented the best of a Southern rural tradition. He was, above all, a man of good will, respected if not loved by those who disagreed with his policies in the valley. Never an intellectual, he was intelligent, high-minded, very concerned with the welfare of the poorer classes in Georgia, sincerely religious and patriotic, intensely loyal to Roosevelt and the New Deal, and always anxious to help the deserving colonists in the valley."

The year after Roosevelt attended the pageant at Pine Mountain Valley, Harry Hopkins transferred the three rural communities over to the Farm Security Agency. Colonists were allowed to buy homes with federal loans. The next year Gay Shepperson left. Defense production and the growth of economic opportunities around Fort Benning at Columbus created jobs that lured colonists out of the community. In 1943 Congress looked into the FSA and concluded that it and the communities were no longer needed. It ordered liquidation. At Pine Mountain Valley, you could buy a nice five-room house with a barn and 30 or 40 acres for $500 down and get a 20- or 30-year loan on the remaining $2,000 at 3 percent interest. The result, 30 years later, is a pleasant, rural, suburban-type community of homeowners, few of them early colonists.

The final balance sheet on Pine Mountain Valley showed that in ten years it cost the federal government $1,400,000 or $7,000 per colonist-family. Straight relief would have been slightly less. Does that mean it was a failure? That depends on what was expected. Roosevelt expected the effort to save money and to bring about a permanent self-sufficient community, neither of which came about. But many lives were improved; hope was kept alive; and it was certainly the sort of gamble worth taking. It *could* have worked. Roosevelt for all his enthusiasm never doubted that this sort of thing was a gamble. "If a community of [this] kind can be made somewhere around 80 per cent self-sufficient," he told reporters in Warm Springs in November 1934, "it probably can be made a go of. But the point is that, obviously, private capital won't go into that. . . . Private capital won't do it because there is too much risk." The government alone was big enough to take such risks.

Tap Bennett stayed to the end, resigning in December 1944. He wanted to stay in Pine Mountain Valley, even then; he bid on the large, handsome manager's home he lived in during his stewardship. His was the high bid, but it was turned down as too low. Henry Kimbrough, a local politician and long-time friend of Roosevelt, as well as a member of the Pine Mountain Valley Community board at one time, urged the President and Hopkins to intervene. On January 5, 1945, Roosevelt wrote Hopkins, "Do you think there is anything we can do?" Nothing was done. It requires no leap of imagination to assume that had Roosevelt not been a dying man trying to manage the greatest war in history, he would have seen to it that his old friend and servant Bennett got what he wanted and deserved.

*A note on sources for this chapter*

Paul Conkin's article, "It All Happened in Pine Mountain Valley," appeared in the *Georgia Historical Quarterly*, March 1963. It is an excellent study of the subject. Tugwell interviewed Tap Bennett at length in the 1950s and the author did in the 1970s. For the general setting necessary to understanding this and other chapters which deal with economic realities of the South in the 1920s and 1930s, *The Emergence of the New South* by George Tindall is quite good.

# The Lessons He Said He Learned

———————◆———————

Roosevelt was forever explaining problems and policies in terms of personal experiences. These anecdotes were so well suited to whatever point he was making at the time that they provoked a fairly widespread suspicion that he was sometimes creative in these endeavors. The ever-skeptical press corps certainly felt that way, and even needled the President about it at times. Once during World War II, Roosevelt explained away charges of inflation by telling the reporters about a "foreman" friend of his who complained about the high cost of living. The President interrogated him and found his complaint was based on the cost of out-of-season strawberries. The President lectured this foreman, or so he told the press, and thus, through the press, the nation.

Later, at a press conference (on May 30, 1944) a question arose regarding raising the price ceilings on certain commodities and textiles. He began a sort of free-association reminiscence about how Georgians wanted higher cotton prices. That led to remarks that he, himself, speaking as a tree farmer, knew that the $29 a thousand-board-feet he was then getting for his lumber in Georgia was a good price, but "thinking personally and selfishly, I would like to see lumber selling at $79 a thousand. Well, I suppose we all have that streak in us. If you pick out cotton, you will have somebody else on your neck, and then—then you will get inflation. But if you do it for one—I suppose one out of ten—you ought to do it for almost anything that grows.

"Substantially, the price that asparagus and some other things bring is a pretty good price, and I know it has made the cost of buying asparagus in the White House awfully high. This is the asparagus season.

"Which reminds me of a friend of mine, a foreman of one of the substantial trades, who came in last January and said to me, 'I have an awful time when I go home.' He says, 'My old lady is ready to hit me over the head with the dishpan.'

"I said, 'What's the trouble?'

" 'The cost of living.'

" 'Well,' I said, 'what, for instance?'

" 'Well, last night I went home and the old lady said, "What's this? I went out to buy asparagus, and do you see what I got? Three sticks. There it is. A dollar and a quarter! It's an outrage." '

"Well, I looked at him, and I said, 'Since when have you been buying asparagus in January—fresh asparagus?'

" 'Oh,' he said, 'I never thought of that.'

" 'Well,' I said, 'tell that to your old lady, with my compliments.' "

A reporter tried to interrupt. "Mr. President, is that—"

Roosevelt continued over the question: "You get a lot of that."

The reporter finished his question: "—is that the same foreman who bought the strawberries in the winter?"

There was what the official stenographer described as "(Much laughter)."

Roosevelt plowed on. "It happened to be a different one, but it's all right. Still marks a true story."

Reporter: "I just wondered if it was the same foreman that came in then." (More laughter)

Judge Rosenman, who wrote many of Roosevelt's speeches, said that the President made up many characters and meetings. Rex Tugwell thought he at least "overworked" his firsthand knowledge of common people, but Tugwell agreed that Roosevelt did in fact learn a great deal from encounters with them in everyday situations—more so in Georgia than in New York. Marvin McIntyre, the President's White House aide, once said, "The story of a farmer who had been ruined by a bank failure, told him at Warm Springs, had much to do with the law insuring bank deposits." In fact, Roosevelt personally knew several Georgia farmers whose lives were greatly harmed, if not actually ruined, by bank failures, including the Doyle family, whose farm he bought. Bank failures began early in Georgia. They were widespread. The Georgia Warm Springs Foundation lost $1,416.09 when the Warm Springs Banking Company suspended operation in 1927. That means Roosevelt lost $1,416.09. He also apparently lost some personal funds the year before when a chain of small Georgia banks, including several in the vicinity, closed. He witnessed a bank failure there even before that.

After 1927, he began banking in Manchester at the bank

of the political operator James Peters. Roosevelt had met Peters earlier and became a regular visitor to steak-dinner seminars at Peters's home. Roosevelt did a lot of listening as the Georgia businessmen discussed their experiences in the local hard times that were a harbinger of national paralysis. He probably did more talking than listening, but, as in his conversation with the foreman about asparagus, both sides undoubtedly learned something.

Roosevelt told people in private meetings as well as in public ones that he learned lessons from simple conversations. Roosevelt once told Fred Botts (according to Turnley Walker), as they relaxed in front of the fireplace in his cottage, "Down here at Warm Springs I can't generalize the way a politician's supposed to. A national problem strikes me as simply people somewhere needing help. What people? Where? What kind of help? . . . The national farm problem? What about Ed Doyle up there on Pine Mountain? The bank? Well, what sort of trouble does Uncle Henry Kimbrough have with his little bank over there in Chipley?"

One of Roosevelt's favorite tales about what he learned in Georgia encounters had to do with education. He told it many times in public and private, for simple as well as sophisticated listeners, varying it a little but not much. This is a 1937 version, from a dedication speech for a black school in Warm Springs.

"It was way back in 1924 [his first visit] that I began to learn economics at Warm Springs. Here is how it happened: One day while I was sitting on the porch of the little cottage in which I lived, a very young man came up to the porch and said, 'May I speak to you, Mr. Roosevelt?' and I said, 'Yes.'

"He came up to the porch and asked if I would come over to such and such a town—not very far away from here—and deliver the diplomas at the commencement exercises of the school.

"I said, 'Yes'; and then I asked, 'Are you the president of the graduating class?' He said, 'No, I am principal of the school.'

'I said, 'How old are you?' He said, 'Nineteen years.'

"I said, 'Have you been to college?' He answered, 'I had my freshman year at the University of Georgia.'

"I said, 'Do you figure on going through and getting a degree?' He said, 'Yes, sir, I will be teaching school every other year and going to college every other year on the proceeds.'

"I said, 'How much are they paying you?' And the principal of that school said, 'They are very generous; they are paying me three hundred dollars a year.'

"Well, that started me thinking. Three hundred dollars for the principal of the school. That means the three ladies who were teaching under him were getting less than three hundred dollars a year. I said to myself, 'Why do they have to pay that low scale of wages? . . . I began realizing that the community did not have any purchasing power. . . .'"

Now, obviously Roosevelt could have learned about the sad state of educational facilities and the lack of purchasing power in the rural South in other ways. But such firsthand experiences were probably better learning experiences. For that matter, he might have been misled about the true state of affairs had he not been the sort to seek out such experiences. He thought so. In 1938 he made another speech in Georgia (at the University in Athens) in which he said this:

"Years ago, when I first came to Georgia, I was told by a

distinguished citizen of the State that public school education was well provided for because there was a law—or
perhaps it was in the State Constitution itself—providing
that every child should have a full school year—and that
attendance for each school year through all the years of
grade school and into the high schools was compulsory. But
I soon discovered—as I might have known that I should—
that school after school in the rural districts of the State—
and most of the districts are rural districts—was open only
four months or five months a year—or was too small to hold
all the children that wanted to go to it, or could not em-
ploy enough teachers—or that children, whose parents who
wanted them to work instead of going to school, could stay
away from school with complete immunity. . . ."

You can be sure that he discovered a lot of that in voy-
ages around the area in his hand-operated autos. It is not
farfetched to speculate that he "learned" over steak at Jim
Peters's that all Georgia children went to school a full term
—then learned in the hard clay front yard of a farm shack
that they didn't.

That he learned from firsthand experiences in New York
is also true, it goes with saying. There were bank failures
in New York when he was Governor which he had to deal
with firsthand. Some rural schools in his native state were
also underfunded and provided poor education. This came
to his attention when he was a state senator. On another
issue, rural electrification and public power, Roosevelt undoubtedly learned plenty from his New York experience.
He had a lengthy, bitter fight over hydroelectric power
while Governor. He lost it, but the utility companies' victory convinced Roosevelt that the way to get cheap power
to the people, particularly in sparsely populated rural areas,

was with federal, rather than just state and local, involvement. However, he claimed that one of the most successful New Deal innovations, the Rural Electrification Administration, was a Georgia baby, born in a cottage in Warm Springs.

"Fourteen years ago," he told a Georgia audience at the dedication of the Lamar County Electric Membership Corporation in 1938, "a Democratic Yankee came to a neighboring county in your state in search of a pool of warm waters wherein he might swim his way back to health. . . . His new neighbors extended to him the hand of genuine hospitality. . . . There was only one discordant note in that first stay of mine at Warm Springs; when the first of the month bills came in for electric light at my little cottage, I found that the charge was 18 cents per kilowatt hour—about four times as much as I paid in Hyde Park. That started my long study of proper utility charges for electricity and the whole subject of getting electricity into farm homes throughout the United States. So it can be said that a little cottage at Warm Springs, Georgia, was the birthplace of the Rural Electrification Administration."

Roosevelt established the REA by executive order in 1935. It was permanent by statute the following year. It provided transmission systems for electric power to communities that private companies would not serve—or would serve only at prohibitive cost. By 1934, Roosevelt's Georgia farm had been electrified. In 1933 the Georgia Power Company, a state private monopoly, agreed to provide the power, providing Otis Moore built his own transmission line. Moore did it at Roosevelt's expense, of course. It cost $351.32. Almost all the cost came for 18 poles at $8.50 each and two miles of copper wire at $140.30.

Most farmers in Georgia, the rest of the South and elsewhere would have been burdened by the expense, but at least some of them could afford it. The cost for poles and wires was much higher when bought from private utilities. Roosevelt explained later how rural property owners (this time in New York, as he described a new cottage he had built in Dutchess County) cut, strip and creosote an "electric pole" for $10, but how a similar pole bought from the power company would cost $40. "That is the whole basis of the REA thing. The REA is being done in large part, of course, by the farmers themselves in a cooperative way."

The situation regarding electric power in Warm Springs was certainly a frustrating one. No wonder Roosevelt learned a lot from it. Not only was power expensive when he first went down—it was extremely unreliable. The night of the season-opening festivities of the Meriwether Inn in 1925, the power failed.

The power in Warm Springs was provided by a local company, which bought its power from a small municipally owned plant in Manchester, five miles away. Roosevelt did not like any of this, and he did not wait till he became President and could launch an REA to do something about it. In 1926, he wrote Thomas Martin, president of the Alabama Power Company, "We in this and neighboring counties are suffering from the usual high costs and inefficient service of small local plants." The Georgia Power Company had recently become affiliated with Alabama Power.

In 1928, the Georgia Power Company bought the Warm Springs distribution system, "partly because of Mr. Roosevelt's urging," according to the company's official history. It reduced the rate from 18 cents per kilowatt hour to about three cents. Later, the rate for the Georgia Warm Springs

Foundation was reduced further. That was in 1929. Basil O'Connor told Preston Arkwright, president of the Georgia Power Company, that Roosevelt would like to talk to him about the rate situation. Arkwright went down to Warm Springs from Atlanta and met Roosevelt and Arthur Carpenter, the foundation's business manager. Roosevelt said he needed a refrigeration plant and a laundry, but could not afford four cents a kilowatt hour for the electricity he thought it would cost for such facilities. Arkwright said the foundation would get its additional electricity at two cents a kilowatt hour, under the schedule that reduced costs as consumption went up.

It was just that sort of improvement in the lives of rural people that Roosevelt had in mind in his fight for cheaper power. Labor-saving devices and other modern technological advances could only bring the march of civilization to farm communities if the people there could afford it. A farmer who could own laundry or refrigeration appliances would be moving to a better life. Roosevelt saw the move as having more than just comfort as a goal. He believed social advancement would follow the electric lines.

Although Roosevelt found the Georgia Power Company generally a forward-looking monopoly, its takeover of the Warm Springs system did not end his problems in the area of his objection to some of its policies and practices. After Georgia Power became responsible for providing the foundation with electricity, Dr. Hubbard occasionally had to call up and ask for extra power so that he could use his new X-ray machine. Also, Roosevelt objected to the way Georgia Power—and all private utilities—figured out their rates. Private utilities were limited to a "reasonable profit" on their assets. Roosevelt often used as an example of how firms inflated their assets a story about the purchase "down in Georgia" of "a run down at the heels municipal plant worth $50,000." Private companies bid for it, pushing the price to $200,000. "Obviously," Roosevelt said, "they should earn a reasonable profit on the $50,000, not the $200,000."

Roosevelt seems to have believed that the REA would not have been necessary but for the excessive economic power of the great utility holding companies. He didn't blame Georgia Power so much as he did its parent organization, Commonwealth and Southern, where he saw an issue that transcended the question of providing electricity to farmers. At a meeting with 35 members of the Associated Church Press in April 1938, the transcript of which was stamped "*Very* Confidential Press Conference," Roosevelt said if Georgians alone could decide, they would extend electric lines to rural areas, but the decision was made at Commonwealth and Southern's headquarters in New York. (The president of the holding company then was Wendell Willkie, who would run against Roosevelt for the presidency in 1940.)

At that meeting with church reporters, Roosevelt followed up his plaint about Commonwealth and Southern with this remark: "One reason for the low wages in pulp mills of Mississippi, Georgia, North Carolina and South Carolina is that practically all profits go North. They do not stay South. If the profits stayed South, the whole scale of living would go up." The question that had set off this remark was: "How great is the danger of fascism in this country?" Roosevelt concluded by saying that there was a tendency to concentrate industrial control in New York. "Now that ultimately is fascism."

So he said he had a *national* reason for wanting to see the South wealthier and more autonomous, as well as the parochial reason that came from being a southerner part of the time: He wanted to see purchasing power grow in Meriwether County, wanted the teachers to be better paid, wanted electricity available to farmers, wanted the local banks insured against failure and takeover in part because it would mean a better life on the scene, and in part because he feared that otherwise economic power would grow to the point that its antidemocratic potential would be too great for a democratic government to oppose.

In early 1938, Roosevelt was approached by Clark Foreman, a liberal adviser to Secretary Ickes, who was paid by the Rosenwald Fund, with the proposal that a special study of the South would draw attention to conditions there and their implication for the nation. Roosevelt agreed and assigned the project to the National Emergency Council, an old New Deal coordinating agency. The NEC convened some southerners in federal service for the study. Roosevelt set the tone in advance of their study by saying he believed the South had become "the nation's number one economic problem—the nation's problem, not merely the South's. For we have an economic unbalance in the nation as a whole, due to this very condition of the South. It is an unbalance that can and must be righted for the sake of the South and of the nation," the President said in July. In August the NEC produced a synopsis of the views of some of the most thoughtful academic students of the southern plight—Rupert Vance and Howard Odum of the University of North Carolina and Walter Prescott Webb of the University of Texas. It blamed the South's sad state on national tariff policy, discriminatory freight rates, monopoly and absentee ownerships.

The report had a strange result. Most southerners who took note of it, it appeared, were upset at what they regarded as criticism of the region, rather than at the northern exploitation that was the clear target of the scholars and Roosevelt. As a political document, it was too abstract.

For Roosevelt, abstract thinking dovetailed with his common sense and neighborly desire to see the depressed South rise again. And not just rise again—but rejoin the rest of the nation as a full partner, economically, emotionally and intellectually. The South had long suffered because of discriminatory freight rates; nonsouthern manufacturers found it attractive to take the region's natural resources out of the South for conversion into consumer items. This tended to keep the South a nonindustrialized region. Roosevelt joined with southern advocates of a national freight-rate structure that would tend to encourage industrial users of southern raw materials to build their plants (thus create well-paying jobs) in the South near those natural resources.

He thought a strong federal government was the best instrument for bringing the South back into the nation. If there were no centralized planning at the national government level, he told a group of visiting British management and labor specialists once, whatever progress had been made in ending sectional differences in the American economy would not have been possible. "I have a place down South," he said. "The whole standard is entirely different. . . . A first-class white carpenter down there [in 1925], he would be glad to take two and a half dollars a day, which was above the standard. He was lucky. He was a millionaire. In our village, he would be a millionaire if he [made] two hundred and fifty dollars a year." New Deal efforts had raised income in Georgia and narrowed the gap, he said.

That was in 1941, but in fact, sectional differences were far from ended. That year, Roosevelt, as President, made another statement to persuade the rest of the nation to provide a special kind of aid to the poor South. He said New York didn't need federal aid for schools but Georgia did. Federal funds for education was an idea that was regarded as quite advanced at that time. Roosevelt had been pushing it. In 1939 Roosevelt had said, "The state[s] of New York, Massachusetts and Illinois ought not to have any aid from the federal government for schools." He was talking to a group of Washington reporters. "But Georgia and Mississippi and Alabama, South Carolina and Arkansas, I think they need aid because they have not got the values down there to build schools and run them. You take the state of Georgia. Some of you were down there with me this year. You remember the Atlanta papers? There were great headlines every morning: 'State Schools Will Probably Close Down the First of January.'

"There is your problem," he said. "We rich people up here, we do not visualize it."

Once when he was advocating industrial incentives in the South, he was criticized on the grounds that manufacturers in New York and New England were being goaded by the federal government to take their jobs to the low-wage South—leaving unemployment behind. He stuck to his guns. He had been referring to "my state of Georgia" for a long time in the South. He often told southern audiences that he was "an adopted son of the South." He began to make similar references on occasions outside the South. "I'm just a Georgia cracker farmer," he said to a large midwestern crowd once. In 1939 he delivered some informal, extemporaneous remarks to the students at Auburn University, in southeastern Alabama, in which he gave a Rooseveltian version of that classic southern complaint about northern exploitation. The Atlanta editor and orator of the 1880s and 1890s, Henry Grady, apostle of the New South, once told of the burial of a Georgian. His clothes, coffin, everything came from outside the region. All Georgia provided was the corpse and the hole in the ground. That was why Georgia was poor.

Roosevelt at Auburn: "The first year I went to Warm Springs, fifteen, nearly sixteen years ago, I had a little cottage that was about a thousand feet from the old A.B.&A. tracks. The first night, the second night and the third night I was awakened out of a deep sleep by the sound of a very heavy train going through at pretty high speed and, as it went through town, the whistle blew and woke everybody up. So I went down to the station and said to the station master, 'What is that train that makes so much noise and why does it have to whistle at half past one in the morning?' 'Oh,' he said, 'the fireman has a girl in town.'

"I asked him what that train was and he said, 'That is the milk train for Florida.' Well, I assumed of course, knowing that the climate of Florida, especially South Florida, is not very conducive to dairy purposes, that this train on the A.B.&A. contained milk and cream from Alabama and Georgia. I was wrong. That milk and cream for Florida came from Wisconsin, Minnesota, Iowa and Illinois and was taken through all the intervening States of Indiana, Ohio, Kentucky, Tennessee, Alabama and Georgia in order to supply milk and cream and butter for Florida.

"That gave me a feeling that something was wrong with the agricultural economy of these States of the lower South, because you and I know from what we have been taught and from the experiments that have been made that these States can produce perfectly good milk and cream.

"A little while later I went down to the village to buy some apples. Mind you, this place is only 75 miles from here. I knew of the magnificent apples raised at the southern end of the Appalachian System. I had tasted them; no apples in the world are better. Yet the apples in Meriwether County, Georgia, the only ones I could find, came from Washington and Oregon.

"I went to buy meat—and I know that we can make pastures in these States—and the only meat that I could buy came via Omaha and Kansas City and Chicago.

"I wanted to buy a pair of shoes and the only shoes I could buy had been made in Boston or Binghamton, New York, or St. Louis.

"Well, that was fifteen years ago, and there wasn't very much change in that system of economy until about six years ago. It was then we began to ask ourselves, 'Why is all this necessary?' I think that we have done more in those six years than in the previous sixty years all through these southern States to make them self-supporting and to give them a balanced economy that will spell a higher wage scale, a greater purchasing power and a more abundant life than they have had in all their history.

"It means a lot of work. It means, incidentally, getting the South 'out of hock' to the North. It means establishing your own enterprises down here with your own capital. I don't believe that the South is so broke that it cannot put its own capital into the establishment of its own enterprises. . . ."

Roosevelt saw promise as well as problems in the South. He foresaw economic progress and growth. Sometimes he sounded like a southern chauvinist; once, for instance, he told an audience that before long the majority of Americans would be "Southerners or descendants of Southerners. . . . Think of that." He also foresaw an eventual end to the South's other great burden, white racism. Some of his critics and even some of his supporters accused him of talking and behaving as if he had adopted his adopted state's views on race relations. That was unfair. But he was no leader on the issue.

In 1940 he was asked by a black student at an off-the-record meeting in Washington to comment on the fact that in the South blacks were not allowed to vote. "And when they try to vote are in some instances, as some of us know, beaten up by thugs and thrown into jail. . . ."

Roosevelt asked him, "What are we going to do about it?" The student asked him the same question. "I will tell you one thing," Roosevelt replied, "you can't change it in the year 1940 or you can't change it in the year 1941. I will give you an illustration: I was in Chattanooga two years ago and I drove around Chattanooga with old Judge—I have forgotten his name—an old Tennesseean.

"We were driving through this street, and if you know your geography, you know the state of Georgia comes right up to the city line of Chattanooga. We were still out in this street, a big wide avenue, in the state of Tennessee, and there was a large portion of the population out in the streets, and they were waving their hats and yelling, 'Hello, Mr. President.'

"I said to the Judge, 'Do these people vote?' 'Yes, there are about 80 percent of them that vote.' I said, 'What? In Tennessee?' He said, 'Sure, not in every part of Tennessee, but they vote in Chattanooga.'

"Then we came to a sign, a little sign, and it said, 'State of Georgia.' We went over past the sign, still in the same suburb, and the colored population was standing there, not saying a word. I said to the Judge, 'You don't vote in Georgia, in this suburb in the same city.' He said, 'No; none vote in Georgia.'

"I said, 'Judge, what is going to happen?' 'Well,' he said,

'there is going to come a time, largely through education.'

"I said, 'How long?' He said, 'I think they will begin voting—it is a gradual process—I think in Georgia they will begin voting in perhaps another five years.'

"I said, 'That is a long ways off.' I said, 'What about the court ruling, the Supreme Court?' He said, 'That is a possibility.' He said, 'I think we have got to pursue all possibilities and bring it along as fast as we can. . . .'

"There is a time element. You cannot get it in one year or two. We are all working and in time it will happen. Of course, part of it is the problem of education and, as you know, in my state of Georgia what education there is is not so hot, poor whites or otherwise."

Roosevelt had not been and was not and would not be working for civil rights in the South. Four years later he made the same little speech to a group of black newspaper publishers. In this version the "colored population" didn't just stand silent; it "showed *no* enthusiasm," he emphasized, with an exaggerated palms-down gesture.

With white journalists, he expressed similar views. At a dinner with members of the American Society of Newspaper Editors in 1938, he was asked if he saw a "growth of racial intolerance." His reply, if publicized, would have put him in the progressive ranks in Georgia. It also demonstrated his understanding of the problem, his empathy, almost, with the racist voters.

"I should say less than there was 10 or 20 years ago," he said. "You and I . . . remember the days of Tom Watson in Georgia. That was an appeal to prejudice. It was an appeal to a very ignorant vote. We have to recognize that fact, because the average boy or girl in my state of Georgia —I am talking about the average in the days of Tom Watson—had no high school and, as far as grade school was concerned, they had an average school year of three or four months. That was the condition. They did not read the daily paper. They did not read a magazine. They were getting the lowest form of pay in the entire nation, and they were therefore completely susceptible to the demagogues. And in Georgia, we have had demagogues, as we all know. You can still have demagogues in Georgia. It is only two or three years since we had Gene Talmadge. He was the red-galluses demagogue. They have had a lot of demagogues in South Carolina. They had old Ben Tillman and they had some since. They have had them in Alabama and a lot of them in Mississippi. They swept the state, Vardaman and all those people. The South, because it is still educationally far behind the rest of the nation, is peculiarly susceptible to the demagogue. Fair? Fair statement?" So he accepted racial demagoguery and worked with the product. He hated the sin but not the sinner.

Throughout his first two terms, not only had Roosevelt refused to work for voting-rights legislation, he had even refused to work for antilynching legislation. He said publicly that he was against lynching and for antilynch legislation in principle, but wasn't sure if it was constitutional. In private, he supported efforts for such a bill, but only in private. When Walter White of the National Association for the Advancement of Colored People asked him to support the legislation in 1934, he refused, saying he needed the help of southern committee chairmen in Congress to pass his New Deal reforms. "I did not choose the tools with [which] I must work," he told White. "If I come out for the anti-lynch bill now, [the southerners] will block every bill I ask Congress to pass to keep America from collapsing. I just can't take that risk." (After 1940 he said he needed them for defense measures.)

Following that meeting with White, Eleanor Roosevelt asked Roosevelt if he objected to her crusading for civil rights legislation. "Do you mind if I say what I think?" she asked. "No, certainly not," he replied. "You can say anything you want. I can always say, 'Well, that is my wife, I can't do anything about her.' "

She took him at his word and became the era's best-known critic of southern racism. She did so in private as well as in public. Once when Walter White complained about the fact that black polio patients were not allowed at Warm Springs, she sent a memo to the President: "They should have a cottage. What is the answer?" Missy LeHand wrote back saying the President didn't want to put anything in writing but would tell White personally that the National Foundation for Infantile Paralysis was going to support separate facilities elsewhere.

Roosevelt's racism was of the benign paternalistic sort that was acceptable to his close friends in Georgia—at least to most of them. He seems not to have ruffled any feathers when he helped to establish "the Warm Springs Negro School" through the Rosenwald Fund (the 5,358th Rosenwald school built in the South). Roosevelt dedicated the school in 1937. According to Mayor W. G. Harry, Roosevelt had initiated the idea in 1933. He had Missy LeHand call the Reverend Mr. Harry and ask him to convene the town's leading businessmen to discuss "a matter of importance." Roosevelt told them, "I'm just embarrassed every time any of my friends comes down here from the North and goes out here and looks at that Negro school building." The difference between it and the white school in those "separate but equal" days was extreme. So a local committee was set up, the Rosenwald officials contacted and the school built.

*Squire* Roosevelt had lent a black farmhand, Mack Cope-land, a considerable amount of money at no interest, had paid the medical expenses of another black man injured while digging a well on his farm, contributed funds to build a new black church in the county. Typical of his paternalism was the way he handled a request from the church. This was in 1937. Reverend C. W. Gamble of the local African Methodist Episcopal Church wrote asking for a contribution. Missy LeHand wrote a reply (with a $10 check) that concluded: "The President also wants me to offer, in all earnestness, the suggestion that every effort should be made to have the colored Baptist denomination worship in the same church with the Methodist—but, of course, suggests separate services as may be desired. . . . Con-tributions for the erection of the building could be received from the members of both churches and the upkeep of one building would, of course, be a great deal less than the upkeep and repairs to two separate buildings." As many well-to-do white southerners would have done, Roosevelt checked out the request with a servant. He sent a memo to his valet McDuffie, who replied, "This is alright. I know the bishop and the board." The valet was not asked if the reply was all right.

It goes without saying that it was a different world then. Roosevelt's property tax returns in Meriwether County were labeled "White Taxpayer" in big letters at the top of the page. There was a white primary election. Some Geor-gia businessmen and politicians complained vehemently when the Works Progress Administration set up a pay schedule which provided blacks *half* as much as whites got.

Roosevelt was at home in Warm Springs, but he was no

racist. Blacks recognized this. They demonstrated this by voting for him. He was the first Democratic presidential candidate to win widespread black support. He carried three out of four black wards in Atlanta in 1932. Blacks could not vote in much of the rural South, but had they been able to, they undoubtedly would have supported him, as the New Deal unfolded. They may have been paid at a discriminatory rate when working on WPA projects, but even that pay meant a great improvement in their lives— and 40 percent of the WPA employees in the state at one time were blacks.

Race was not an issue in the minds of most white voters then, however racist they might have been. Roosevelt carried the Solid South every time he ran. He won in Georgia by margins ranging from 5 to 1 to 12 to 1. In his four presidential campaigns he won in Meriwether County by margins of from 12 to 1 to 50 to 1. (He never carried Dutchess County.) This popularity fooled him—and led him down the path to a humiliating political defeat.

## *A note on sources for this chapter*

*In Search of Roosevelt* and *The Brains Trust*, both by Rex Tugwell, were used in this chapter. So was *Working with Roosevelt* by Samuel Rosenman and *A Man Called White* by Walter White. *The History of the Georgia Power Company* by Wade Wright was also used.

# The Effectiveness of His Frown

Sanford Football Stadium in Athens, Georgia, a natural bowl with seating on a perfectly inclined hillside. It was August 11, 1938. A brutal late morning sun blazed out of a cloudless sky on 15,000 Georgians come to see the seniors, graduate students and dignitaries receive their degrees.

A platform had been set up in the center of the football field, to which a procession of men and women marched, sweltering in academic robes. The sheriff of the county led the procession in a tight-fitting tailcoat and red sash. Fifteen hundred 4-H Club girls in bright green dresses with green feathers added a festive note to the August assemblage. It was a stirring scene—but not stirring enough to have attracted 15,000 Georgians out in the midday heat. The real attraction was the President of the United States, come to accept an honorary degree and make a speech. Roosevelt was finishing up an unprecedented political campaign by a President. He had journeyed across the continent urging voters to support his friends in Congress. Now he was about to urge them to defeat his enemies.

It was widely known in Georgia, indeed in the nation, that he regarded the senior senator from Georgia, Walter F. George, as a foe of the first water. Since George was an incumbent, a power in the Senate, and since Georgia was Roosevelt's adopted home, the fight over George's bid for renomination made the Democratic primary there more charged than any of the other primary battles Roosevelt was "meddling" in, and certainly more charged than any previous primary fight in Georgia. The crowd knew where Roosevelt stood. He had said the day before at Warm Springs that he hoped George would be defeated.

Organ music blared to fill the time as the dignitaries and crowd waited for Roosevelt. He arrived 15 minutes late in a Secret Service car with the Governor of the state, the chancellor and president of the university. He walked stiffly up a ramp to the stand on an aide's arm. He posed for photographers as the black robe was put over his shoulders. Then he began a speech about how much he had learned firsthand in Georgia about its poverty—and how important it was for Georgians to support the national government's efforts to raise purchasing power in the South. Those in the audience who came hoping to hear him attack Senator George, or another candidate in the race, former Governor Eugene Talmadge, or to endorse his own chosen candidate, the United States Attorney in Atlanta, Lawrence Camp, were disappointed. He mentioned no names, though he alluded to the two opponents when he said in conclusion, "At heart, Georgia shows devotion to the principles of democracy. Georgia, like other states, has occasional lapses; but it really does not believe either in demagoguery or feudalism, even though they are dressed up in democratic clothes." Talmadge was an extreme racist, even measured against the standards of the day in the South, and George, as Roosevelt had hinted in an earlier Georgia speech, was a feudalist in his eyes.

Reporters at Athens knew that Roosevelt planned to attack George by name later in the day in a speech at nearby Barnesville. And one there wrote of the Athens speech that Roosevelt "seemed eager to be on his way. Indeed, near the end of speech he seemed to be wishing he could say the names then and there and not wait for Barnesville in the afternoon."

The "purge" campaign trip had begun for Roosevelt less than two months before, when he delivered a radio fireside chat to the nation in which he charged that many Democrats who had been elected, as he had, to carry out liberal policies were not supporting him in his efforts to achieve such a goal. Democratic votes defeated several Roosevelt measures in Congress in 1937 and 1938. So, he said, Democrats who supported him would get his active support against Democrats who did not in the summer primaries. Then he took off on a trip that would take him into Ohio, Kentucky, Indiana, Arkansas, Oklahoma, Texas, Colorado, Nevada and California, before he came back to campaign in Georgia, South Carolina and Maryland. In the states he spoke in before he came to Georgia, he endorsed incumbent senators, or stayed aloof, but in Georgia, South Carolina and Maryland, he would try to topple incumbents.

The fireside chat and the cross-country train trip were

not the real beginnings of the campaign. In both Alabama and Florida, incumbent New Dealers who had been appointed to the Senate faced tough challenges early in the year. Lister Hill, with FDR's support, defeated Thomas J. Heflin, in Alabama in January; and Claude Pepper, with an FDR nod, defeated two opponents in May. "You have been vindicated by the people of Florida," that state's Governor wired Roosevelt. Pepper had supported Roosevelt on the controversial legislation that would have allowed the President to add New Deal supporters to the Supreme Court without waiting for some of the conservative justices to retire. It was that defeat that symbolized Roosevelt's worsening relations with Congress in 1937 and touched off the purge attempt.

Buoyed by these two victories in states neighboring Georgia, Roosevelt decided to take on Walter George. He had been wanting to do it at least since the previous fall. In November 1937, while riding to Miami in his train, he and Interior Secretary Harold Ickes discussed creating a new liberal party organization in the deep South. As the train sped through Georgia, Roosevelt said he would like to set up in Georgia and South Carolina "progressive Democratic organizations . . . which will at least divide the control in those states." Ickes said it would be good if George and Senator E. D. Smith of South Carolina could be beaten.

In January, Roosevelt called in an old Georgia friend, L. W. (Chip) Robert, who was then assistant to the Secretary of the Treasury and treasurer of the Democratic party, and suggested he run against George. Robert was a wealthy builder and a member of the Atlanta business establishment that Walter George was so intimately involved with.

(George was asked once if he wasn't too closely tied to the Georgia Power Company. Rather than denying it, as most politicians would have, he said he was proud to be close to big businesses such as the power company.) Robert refused, but agreed to go to Georgia to start seeking support for a possible purge. He was laughed at, cursed, hung up on by his old friends.

About that same time, the end of January 1938, James Roosevelt telephoned James Farley to ask about an official party statement on the primaries. The young Roosevelt was serving as a political aide in the White House. Farley, Postmaster General and chairman of the party, dictated a statement on the primaries, which concluded: "These nominations are entirely the affairs of the state or the congressional districts, and however these early battles may result the National Committee will be behind the candidates that the people themselves choose. This goes for every state and every congressional district." Ten minutes later Farley's phone rang. It was James. "Father has struck the last two sentences out," he said. Subsequently, the President told Farley he wanted to defeat George and a handful of other members of Congress—some of whom, it turned out, did not have opposition.

In March Roosevelt went to Warm Springs for a week's rest. En route his train stopped at the north Georgia town of Gainesville. It had been devastated by a tornado, then rebuilt with federal aid. Roosevelt delivered a major speech in the newly named Roosevelt Square to a crowd of some 20,000 townsfolk and visiting mountaineers and farmers. The *New York Times* called the audience "the greatest turnout ever given him by a Southern community during his years at the White House." He had spoken to larger southern audiences before, but the 20,000 in Roosevelt Square represented double the town's population.

Roosevelt had also spoken to more enthusiastic audiences. He received relatively little applause and few cheers. The reason given to the press by some Democrats was that north Georgians were typically reserved. The more likely answer was that Roosevelt's speech appeared to be an attack on Georgia (thus the Gainesville reaction was a portent of the Southwide reaction that would greet the "economic problem number one" report later that summer). He said the "lower South" had such meager purchasing power, because of low wages, that it "cannot and will not" establish "successful new industries." He said his administration was trying to help the South and poor persons elsewhere, but was being held back by "selfishness on the part of a few." He said such people still believed in the feudal system, which he compared to fascism. To such people "in and out of public office, who still believe in the feudal system . . . the people of the United States and every section of the United States are going to say, 'We are sorry but we want people to represent us whose minds are cast in the 1938 mold. . . .'"

That was a clear challenge to Walter George, who had introduced Roosevelt in Gainesville. He sat in a silence deeper than the crowd's for this veiled attack. The veil was diaphanous to all who were paying any attention to politics that year. Vice President John Garner told Farley at a lunch in the Capitol shortly thereafter that the speech was a disaster. "The boss has stirred up a hornet's nest by getting into their primary fights. There are now twenty Democrats in the Senate who will vote against anything because they are mad clear through."

There was still no anti-George candidate at that time. Chip Robert and other Roosevelt lieutenants were having trouble finding a candidate, because George was so strong. Eugene Talmadge was thought certain to be a candidate, but he was blatantly anti-Roosevelt, as well as being a thoroughly discredited racist demagogue. "I'm going to endorse someone, if I have to pick my tenant farmer Moore," Roosevelt told Farley that spring.

In May, on the heels of the Pepper victory in Florida, the die was cast—if it hadn't always been—and at a strategy session involving Ickes, James Roosevelt and others, it was agreed to go into Georgia. The decision was not publicized, and some Georgians got the idea that Roosevelt had concluded not to challenge George. That was on the 9th. On the 14th, Lawrence Camp wired Roosevelt, "The friends in Georgia of the President . . . wonder if he is correctly informed as to the political situation here. Georgia is much more pro-Roosevelt than Florida and the coming Georgia primary furnishes the administration its opportunity to gain real friends and supporters in Congress." And so Camp, who was "100 per cent for the New Deal," was selected. By whom is not quite clear. Both Chip Robert and Marvin McIntyre of the White House staff have been given credit. Camp was a poor candidate, but the single potentially strong candidate was Governor E. D. Rivers, who was also a New Dealer and quite popular—and who wasn't interested, preferring the easier campaign to win another term in the State House.

Roosevelt finished his train campaign in California and returned through the Panama Canal to Pensacola, Florida, by Naval vessel. Thence to Warm Springs, where on August 10 he remarked casually to some patients and staff members of the foundation that Lawrence Camp, seated there with him for lunch, was "a gentleman who I hope will be the next senator from this state." Until then there were still some who didn't believe the President would put his own prestige on the line against the venerable George. At that moment, his Barnesville speech had not been written. He would dictate it that afternoon at Warm Springs.

That day he had received word that an incumbent senator he had backed—in Idaho—had lost a primary fight. But that was the first such defeat. Elsewhere he had been victorious. He prepared to go on to Athens—and Barnesville. "The Roosevelt smile of approval for favored senators has seemingly exerted strong influence on many Democratic voters in this campaign," an Associated Press reporter wrote after the Warm Springs lunch, "and now the effectiveness of his frown is to be tested."

If a crowd of 20,000 in Gainesville in March was worthy of note, then the crowd that began to stream into little Barnesville in August was truly remarkable. Barnesville was a military-college town of only 3,000 population. Early that morning, while Roosevelt was still en route to Athens, crowds began to arrive. Eventually 25,000 to 30,000 Georgians would fill the Gordon Military Institute stadium and spill over onto red clay banks.

The occasion for the speech was the beginning of electric service to rural customers of a cooperative made possible by the Rural Electrification Administration. Roosevelt was to throw the switch. He had been invited—by Lawrence Camp—to speak "on any subject you may deem of interest to Georgians." That was in early July. George supporters thought that too obvious an appeal for a political speech, and a week before the August 11 date they prevailed upon the rural electric group of Barnesville to issue a statement urging "all candidates and friends of candidates to refrain from campaigning in Lamar County and to refrain from use of partisan banners and posters until after the President's visit. . . ."

It was clear by then that the dedication was going to be political, one way or the other. George was going to appear on the speaker's platform. So was Camp. Talmadge was not. Camp had assured a Camp crowd by sending out invitations to 12,000 supporters.

It was as hot and bright in Barnesville as it had been in Athens. An occasional breeze gave some relief to the dusty crowd—relief and even delight, as the fragrance of peach trees and pine wafted through the heated air. The speaker's stand was of newly cut raw pine, and glared white and yellow in the sun. The scene was almost too dramatic. It seemed staged. Though candidate Camp and Governor Rivers and Senator Richard Russell and other distinguished men were on the stand, all eyes were on the President and Senator George. The former had on a double-breasted tropical suit of such a light gray color as to seem almost white. He was smiling as he began to speak. George, somber, occasionally frowning, sat in a dark suit, one leg crossed over the other.

The President spoke hurriedly about rural electrification. He turned then to his theme about the need for liberal Democrats in Congress. "The man who says he is for progress but whose record shows that he hinders or hampers or tried to kill new measures of progress" is "dangerous," Roosevelt said. The crowd knew whom he meant. So did the senator. He took a piece of paper out of his pocket and began to write on it as Roosevelt continued.

"You, the people of Georgia, in the coming senatorial primary . . . have a perfect right to choose any candidate you wish . . . but because Georgia has been good enough to call me her adopted son and because for many long years I have regarded Georgia as my 'other state,' I feel no hesitation in telling you what I would do if I could vote here next month. . . ."

The crowd was getting restless and noisy. Roosevelt digressed about his opponents in Congress. "What I am about to say," he continued—and a voice from the crowd came: "We know what you are going to say!" as if imploring him to get on with it—"will be no news to my old friend . . . Senator Walter George. . . . Let me make it clear that he is, and I hope will always be, my personal friend. He is beyond question a gentleman and a scholar—" The rural Georgians drowned him with cheers for George. "—but," Roosevelt continued, "with whom I differ heartily and sincerely on the principles and policies of how the government of the United States ought to be run."

Over the crowd's buzz, Roosevelt turned to the other candidates. Talmadge, who was not on the pine stand, and whose advocates were not in the dusty audience, he dismissed as one "who concerns me not at all." This brought the loudest boos, cheers and laughter of the day. It was the one thing the Camp, George and Roosevelt supporters all were agreed on. As to Camp, Roosevelt said, "I have known him for many years. He has had experience in the State Legislature; he has served as Attorney General of Georgia and for four years, he has made a distinguished record in the United States District Court, his office ranking among the first two in the whole of the United States in the expedition of federal cases in that court. I regard him not only as a public servant with successful experience but as a man who honestly believes that many things must be done and done now to improve the economic and social conditions of the country, a man who is willing to fight for those objectives. . . .

"Therefore, answering the requests that have come to me from many leading citizens of Georgia that I make my position clear, I have no hesitation in saying that if I were able to vote in the September primaries in this state, I most assuredly should cast my ballot for Lawrence Camp. . . ."

The roar from Camp and George supporters drowned out most of the anticlimactic closing remarks. As soon as the President finished, friends of George on the platform rushed to him as they would to a stricken man, but he leapt from his wooden cane-bottomed chair to grasp Roosevelt's hand. As they shook, George said, "Mr. President, I regret that you have taken this occasion to question my democracy and to attack my public record. I want you to know that I accept the challenge!"

"God bless you, Walter. Let's always be friends."

Then the President left the stand and he and his party left the primary stage to the combatants.

At least, physically he did. In fact, the contest in the month that remained before the primary was pure George and Roosevelt. George was the only candidate that really mattered. And Roosevelt was the only issue.

When the President attacked George for his behavior in Congress, he was reacting to the Georgian's votes on a few key Roosevelt measures—the Public Utility Holding Company Act, the Wagner Housing Act, government reorganization and, principally, the wages and hours bill. But George had voted for many key Rooseveltian proposals. He supported the Tennessee Valley Authority, the National Labor Relations Act, the Agricultural Adjustment Act, Social Security, the Securities and Exchange Commission, the National Recovery Administration. He was a thoroughgoing conservative, an ally of big business, more and more after 1936, but he was no reactionary or one-dimension puppet of the special interests. In fact, George often called himself an advocate of "liberal democracy."

And so Camp was correct in saying that "If you want to help the President, vote for me." He was, as he said often, "100 per cent for the New Deal." But it was not correct to say, as he also did often, "The issues in this campaign are clear and simple: do we want to go along with a national program or do we want to go back to the days when the program of the national government was only to help big business?" If it had been that simple, then George might have lost. You have to say "might have," because George did a masterful job of diverting the public's attention from any substantive, legislation-related issues. He made the issue Roosevelt's intervention in the race.

"The people of Georgia do not need to be told by the President of the United States whom to vote for. That is their business. We are capable of managing our affairs without outside help from the President." Roosevelt had a home in Georgia, of course, but George took that head on, too. "I'm a Georgian bred and born," he told one audience after Barnesville. "I'm a full-time Georgian, too!" Nor did the senator make Roosevelt the only meddler. In a major speech shortly after Barnesville, in the tobacco town of Waycross in far southeast Georgia, he attacked White House advisers "Tommy Corcoran and Benny Cohen, two little Wall Street lawyers who had arrogated to themselves the power of saying who shall be senator and who shall not be senator." (Corcoran, in fact, may well have been the man behind the purge.) He also attacked John L. Lewis and "James Ford, the Negro nominee of the Communist party for vice president," and E. L. Oliver of the "so-called Non-Partisan League," who "demanded that I vote for the reorganization of the judicial branch of the government."

Walter George was a dignified country gentleman who had to be chauffeured everywhere because he never learned to drive a car. Whereas Eugene Talmadge, the third candidate in the race, was famous for his personal attacks on his opponents, George was famous for not making speeches of any sort in his own behalf. He had not had to make a stump speech since the 1926 Senate race. In 1932 he had no opposition. Talmadge's style was to take off his coat (displaying his trademark, red galluses) and roll up his sleeves before his tirades. On the hottest Georgia day, according to legend, George would not even *unbutton* his coat for a speech, outdoors or in.

So his heated campaign rhetoric was a surprise to many Georgians. He stuck to his theme. If Walter George got beat, Georgians would be submitting to outside meddling.

Yankee outside meddling. "The purge," he said, "is a second march through Georgia." An antilynch bill pending in the Senate was "carpet-baggery glorified." Margaret Mitchell, the author of *Gone with the Wind*, a supporter of George, wrote a friend that "since Roosevelt's Barnesville speech Senator George and his supporters have been on the air. I have heard so many yells of 'states rights' and 'Northern oppression' and 'sinister centralization of power' and so many bands playing 'Dixie' that I have wondered whether this was 1938 or 1861." Miss Mitchell wrote Connecticut friends two weeks before primary election day that "for the first time in more years than I can remember there's a real issue in Georgia politics. . . . People who were for Roosevelt before go around muttering, 'I'm damned if any Yankee is going to tell me how to mark my ballot!' "

She also wrote that she was fearful the senator and Talmadge would end up dividing the "conservative" vote. A number of people believed this would occur to Camp's benefit. However, it was clear to the most astute observers, including Roosevelt, that Camp wasn't going to win anything. Candidate Camp, Bill Flythe of Augusta wrote Marvin McIntyre at the end of August, was as lackluster as Alf Landon had been in the presidential race of two years before. (Alf Landon, the Republican nominee, won just two out of 48 states, in the worst American presidential defeat up to that time.) Furthermore, he had no organization. Roosevelt's hopes that Governor Rivers's organization would work for him as it worked to reelect (renominate, technically) Rivers were dashed. Many elements of the Rivers organization worked for George. Republican officials in the state came out openly for George, with the goal of embarrassing Roosevelt and dividing the Democratic party in 1940. Republicans could vote in the Democratic primary since there was no party registration. White Republicans, that is. Though Camp had been regarded as a "labor man" since his days in the legislature, labor's leaders in the state and nation were split, with George getting much open support.

The only thing Camp had going for him was the federal bureaucracy. Roosevelt saw to it that top officials of the Department of Agriculture made speeches in Camp's behalf. Officials in several New Deal agencies in Georgia were allowed or told to work for Camp. Before the Barnesville speech, WPA wages were increased in the South. Two days after Barnesville, the WPA announced $1.8 million in Georgia projects; on August 23, $1.7 million more. In September there was a smaller grant of $101,000 plus a PWA grant of $819,000 plus an announcement that the state was going to get $990,000 for highways.

There was negative aid from Washington, too. Erle Cocke, state director of the National Emergency Council and regional director of the Reconstruction Finance Commission, was a George man. He was replaced in late July by Clark Foreman. Edgar Dunlop, the state's Reconstruction Finance Commission attorney, was forced to resign when he sided with George. Even lower-level aides were being caught in the crossfire, according to George supporters. A secretary at the NEC was fired, according to her father, Charles Rountree, a weekly newspaper editor in Wrightsville, because his paper wouldn't support Camp.

A special Senate committee investigated these and other charges and found nothing specific it could act on. The

Hatch Act, forbidding federal employees to participate in politics, was the eventual result of such behavior, however.

As far as Camp was concerned, the Roosevelt machine did not enforce enough loyalty in 1938. After the election, he complained that the acting manager of the RFC in Atlanta, the state director of the Federal Housing Administration, the regional director of the Federal Deposit Insurance Corporation, the Atlanta Federal Reserve Board chairman, the collector of the Port of Savannah and other federal officials all had worked for George. Not a one was dismissed.

One casualty of the purge effort was Elsie O'Neal, the ordinary of Meriwether County. A long-time Roosevelt supporter, she backed Camp. In early 1940 she was defeated in a bid for return to office. That spring she went to the temporary White House in Warm Springs, which was always set up on Roosevelt visits, and asked for a federal job. McIntyre told James Rowe, a staff member who handled political matters, "the President rather emphatically said that he wanted something done." She eventually was found a job as an area supervisor in the Historical Records Project of the WPA in Columbus.

Roosevelt often took an interest in patronage matters in Meriwether County. An effort that had not turned out too well was the one long before the 1938 election, which got a part-time RFC job for Judge Henry Revill of Greenville. Revill was a genial 300-pound lawyer and the publisher of the *Meriwether Vindicator*, probably the first paper to propose a Roosevelt presidency. In 1938, Revill was also on retainer to the Georgia Power Co. He supported George. W. E. Irvin, a justice of the peace in Greenville and a

Roosevelt loyalist (and Camp supporter), complained about Revill's behavior in the primary to McIntyre, who proposed to FDR in a memo that Jesse Jones, head of the RFC, fire Revill. The memo came back from FDR with the pencil notation, "Mac, Yes, will you do it."

The final nail in Camp's coffin was money. George's campaign chests bulged with aid from utility officers and other conservatives. He spent over $44,000. Camp spent $17,000. Talmadge spent just under $9,000. These are the special committee's figures. Georgia politicians estimated privately that the totals were much higher—and even more in George's favor.

When the votes were counted, George had won with 141,000 votes to Talmadge's 103,000 to Camp's 77,000 (all rounded). In Georgia primaries then, each county, regardless how small, cast at least two unit votes in convention; no matter how populous, the large counties cast only six unit votes each. The system assured rural dominance. George won across the board, with 242 unit votes to Talmadge's 148 and Camp's 20. Talmadge tried to reverse the vote by getting recounts in many counties, but was rebuffed. Then he tried to manipulate the convention and was again rebuffed.

In Meriwether County, Roosevelt was also rebuffed. Camp came in third there.

Why did Roosevelt do it? There are at least four plausible explanations: (1) He simply disliked George, despite what he said at Barnesville. He certainly disapproved of him. Though George had voted for many New Deal programs, he had not only voted against some key ones, he had also served on the ad hoc steering committee in the Senate that led the fight to kill the court reorganization bill. Even before that, Roosevelt had become upset with George's record. In 1928 he wrote Al Smith's preconvention campaign manager that a southerner ought to be on the ticket. He said he preferred Cordell Hull. George, he said, "has made a few mistakes in the past few months."

(2) He thought he could win. Roosevelt was enormously popular in Georgia and so were his programs. Public-opinion polls showed that. His birthday was a legal holiday there. The state Senate approved the court bill. So did referenda in several counties. The AAA was more popular in Georgia than in almost any other state. When he was asked at an American Society of Newspaper Editors dinner in April of 1938 if he expected the South to remain "solid," he replied, "I think the South is going to remain Democratic but I think it is going to be a more intelligent form of Democracy. . . . It is going to be a liberal Democracy." He was misled by the personal adulation he enjoyed in his adopted state.

(3) He thought *Talmadge* could win. Roosevelt and most of his inner circle despised Talmadge and all he stood for. "I think he is one of the most contemptible figures in public life," Ickes confided to his diary in 1936. But a Talmadge in the Senate would be preferable to a George. George could win battles there with his growing institutional power, and his ability to lead undecided senators. Talmadge would be just one vote—and his antics might even turn undecided senators toward Roosevelt on specific issues. In May 1938, A. B. Lovett, a strong FDR man and

astute Georgia political insider who had been Richard Russell's campaign manager in his successful 1938 Senate race, wired Roosevelt that he would risk electing Talmadge if he supported a third candidate. James Roosevelt got the wire and asked James Farley how to respond. Farley said, "Don't," but undoubtedly one or the other told the President about the appeal. The next month, Roosevelt had a conference with Chip Robert, who made a last plea to sidetrack the Georgia purge. "If you do come [to Georgia] and use your influence to beat George, Gene Talmadge will beat him. I can't conceive of your wanting Gene Talmadge to come to Washington as a senator. . . . You can't let Gene Talmadge put on the show he'd put on. He'd be a menace."

Roosevelt replied, "Yes, I'd prefer that."

(4) He was interested in the state—and the South—being liberal and not being solid. He wanted to demonstrate a base of liberal voters that would make conservative congressmen think before voting against him. In a sense, he did demonstrate that there was a liberal feedback in Georgia. Considering that Camp was a poor campaigner, underfinanced, underorganized; and considering that Roosevelt's entry stirred up even some of his liberal supporters in nativist wrath (even the *Atlanta Constitution* denounced him); and considering that it was a *white* primary, thus one in which the most liberal voices were stifled; and, finally, considering that Georgia was a poll-tax state in which those poorest whites who were likely to support a liberal federal administration's policies and champions (when no race issue was involved) were also stifled—considering all that, the fact that Camp got even a fourth of the vote in a three-man race was something.

# A note on sources for this chapter

*The Wild Man of Sugar Creek* by William Anderson is a good biography of Eugene Talmadge, with much material on the 1938 campaign. Margaret Mitchell's *Gone with the Wind Letters*, edited by Richard Harwell, offers several glimpses of the year's background. *Jim Farley's Story* by James Farley deals with the period of the purge. "Senator Walter George's 1938 Campaign" by Luther H. Zeigler, Jr., appeared in the December 1959 issue of the *Georgia Historical Quarterly* and is a good, detailed examination. Also quite useful is *Franklin D. Roosevelt and the Primary Campaigns of the 1938 Congressional Elections* by A. Blair Crownover.

# A Pool and Some Whispers

"The greatest calamity to this country is that President Roosevelt can't walk around and hunt up people to talk to," Eugene Talmadge told the *New York Times* in 1935. "The only voice to reach his wheelchair were the cries of the 'gimme crowd.'" That was not the only time Talmadge attacked Roosevelt in public in connection with lameness. Once he said the people couldn't respect "a man who can't walk a two by four." After Roosevelt was elected President he became the target of such arrows by his most extreme critics. Some were in public, like the Talmadge statements, but most were in private. Roosevelt was subjected to the most vicious whispering campaign in modern American political history. But practically none of this got into the papers. Neither was there much straight news reporting or disinterested analysis dealing with his affliction. There were absolutely no photographs or movie newsreels depicting him as a cripple. Much of the American public never thought of him as disabled. That is true, even though one of the first great newspaper campaigns dealing with Roosevelt in the White House dealt with his lameness. And it is true even though Roosevelt used his office and his history to publicize the effort to find a cure for polio.

That first campaign had to do with getting a swimming pool built in the White House. Roosevelt had, of course, turned to swimming for therapy and recreation shortly after he was stricken. He had the pools at Warm Springs, at his family estate in Hyde Park and at the Governor's Mansion in Albany. But there were no convenient facilities for him in Washington.

The *New York Daily News,* the highly successful tabloid whose publisher, Captain Joseph Patterson, was a Roosevelt backer then, decided to remedy that. On March 14, 1933, ten days after Roosevelt took the oath, the *News* splashed four pictures of Roosevelt on its front page. The cutlines said "Help build a pool for Roosevelt. Franklin D. Roosevelt (above) who is leading the country out of depression, must have a pool for his health. There is none at the White House. Therefore, today *The News* undertakes to act as medium for citizens of New York State to express affection for F.D. by giving him a pool." One of the pictures showed Roosevelt in a pool. On page 3 the campaign continued, with another picture of Roosevelt, this time playing water football, a large headline "ALL NEW YORK TO BUY F.D. SWIMMING POOL," and a story that described the presidential lameness in the baldest terms of any story in a general-circulation newspaper. "Swimming, as has been said, is the President's only sport. The other diversion is reading. He can't ride horseback, as have so many of his predecessors. He cannot, actually, go outdoors at all for any distance, except in an automobile.

"The water is his one form of healthful recreation. He's lost without it. It's the very essence of his existence. It is, in fact, in the long run, his life. It was swimming coupled with the President's magnificent courage and will that enabled him to win his battle with infantile paralysis." With magnificent irrationality, the story said the pool was going to be a surprise for the President.

The *News* estimated the pool would cost $15,000. The next day there was a story about how the money was already coming in—$1,304.43. But $1,000 of that was donated by the *News*. Also that day the paper had an editorial in support of its own drive—the job was a mankiller and FDR had to be kept healthy, it said—and began printing coupons for donors to use. On the 16th: "It's F.D. Landslide. . . ." The total was $8,729.47, but that included "services"of an architect and an accounting firm that volunteered to audit the swimming pool fund. The 18th: $12,995.41. The story that day told of an eight-year-old in Queens who donated 25 cents he was saving for a pony. By the 21st, the *News* was saying $16,676.32—much of that in services—had been contributed. It was publishing the names and amounts of all contributors down to a dime. It announced that day that 100 "Broadway celebrities" would perform in a midnight benefit at the Capitol Theater to put the fund over the top.

"Thanks Everybody; F.D. Gets His Swimmin' Pool" was the headline March 25. "*The News* today closed its contribution list." The grand total was $21,829.69, counting services that would not directly underwrite the pool itself. The cash total was just over $12,000 and the *News* estimated that donations in the mail plus proceeds from the benefit would more than cover the $15,000 check it was preparing to write for the federal construction team headed by Lieutenant Colonel U.S. Grant III.

The show netted some $8,000. Tickets cost $1.10 to $3.30, for which the swimming pool subsidizers got quite a treat: James Melton, Irving Berlin, Clayton, Jackson and Durante, Bea Lillie, Alfred Lunt and Lynn Fontanne, Noel Coward, Frances Lederer and Dorothy Gish, Fred Astaire, Eddie Duchin, Gilda Gray, Stoopnagle and Budd, Lupe Velez, Edward G. Robinson, Bette Davis, Joan Blondell, Lilly Damita, Tallulah Bankhead, Vincent Lopez, Pat Rooney, Sr. and Jr., Eugenie Leontovich, Ethel Merman, Jack Dempsey, the Street Singer, Fanny Brice, Jack Benny, Ted Lewis, Bert Lahr, Borrah Minnevich, Little Jack Little and at least a dozen more well-known show-business personalities. The event was the prototype of later fund raising by show-business stars for political parties and candidates.

John Roosevelt attended in person. The President listened to a special radio broadcast over New York station WMCA. He wired the theater, "Broadcast splendid. I enjoyed it."

Colonel Grant meanwhile began planning. He thought at first Roosevelt wanted a small exercise pool and requested blueprints of pools and work tables from Warm Springs. Roosevelt said he wanted a pool to swim in. Given the choice of indoors or out, he chose in. His first problem was the cost. It appeared when bids were sought that Grant would have only about $20,000 in cash. Even though the federal government was going to do the demolition and earthwork to create a basement under the White House for the pool, the three construction companies bid $23,477, $25,700 and $26,728. A good bit more than the $15,000 original estimate. The pool was not a large one—15x51 feet, with a maximum depth of seven and a half feet. But the pool room and dressing rooms, with elaborate tilework, added greatly to the cost. The first low bidder reworked its proposal to get it down to $19,995.15. Roosevelt followed the planning closely, once arguing with Grant in favor of cheap plaster rather than tile. Condensation problems required a compromise—glazed terra-cotta in some places, crab-orchard stone elsewhere. The final cost of the pool was $22,316.64.

On June 3, the *News* proudly ran a picture of the pool on its front page. "You gave this to the President," a line said. A story quoted Roosevelt: "I just want to say one personal word of thanks to [workmen] top to bottom. I admire the fine spirit that all displayed in building this fine pool. The pool is of inestimable benefit and swimming in it is the only exercise I can get."

The next day, a Saturday, he and Eleanor took their first dip in the pool. Thereafter, a 5:30 P.M. swim became a Roosevelt routine when he was in residence at the White House. That, stretching exercises, and massages by Commander George Fox, a Navy officer attached to the White House as aide to the President, became the major therapy for Roosevelt in his presidential years. His trips to Warm Springs averaged barely over one a year after he became President, and he did not get into the pool on the briefest of those. Fox, by the way, did not come to the White House to be Roosevelt's masseur. He had served as an aide to Calvin Coolidge and Herbert Hoover.

The press had little to say about Roosevelt's lameness thereafter. During his twelve years as President, there was a conspiracy engaged in by the President, the White House staff, the Secret Service and the journalists who wrote about, broadcast about and took still and moving pictures of Roosevelt. He was never—well, hardly ever—described as crippled, as unable to walk except with extreme effort and braces and other assistance. Photographers were informed on arriving at the White House that no pictures of the President being carried by a bodyguard or in any other posture that showed him helpless or undignified were allowed. That included shots of Roosevelt in his wheelchair. "You were requested, not ordered, to refrain from taking pictures of this type," Murray Alvey of Pathe, a newsreel outfit, said. So did Frank Cancallare of Acme, a service that provided still pictures for newspapers. But it was still more than a request. The first day he was assigned to the White House, Cancallare said, Steve Early, the President's press secretary, asked him not to take such pictures. "It's an unwritten rule," he said. The photographer asked his colleagues and found this was true. And it went beyond that, really. Hugo Johnson, of Paramount News, said he was told by a Secret Service agent never to turn his movie camera on while the President was in motion. The agent said he would take his film away if he did.

Rarely, a photographer assigned to the White House, or —less rarely—one covering a presidential event for the first time, would train his camera on the President in a forbidden pose. A staff aide or a Secret Service agent spotting that would say, "No pictures." On at least one occasion, Cancallare recalled later, a still photographer ignored the agent and took a picture. The standard press camera then was the Speed Graphic, which had holders for individual film plates rather than spools of film. On that occasion when his command was ignored, the agent walked over to the photographer and yanked the plate from the holder.

One picture of Roosevelt being pushed in his wheelchair did appear in *Life* magazine in 1937, but he and his attendants are in the deep background of the photograph, a mere half-inch tall, and the picture conveys no sense of disability. Murray Alvey once took a very long shot of Roosevelt being wheeled into the Waldorf Astoria for a campaign appearance. He was shooting the entry of other notables and was surprised to see Roosevelt appear. No agents noticed, or at least none made an effort to take his film. He sent it in to his editors. It was never used. On occasion photos showing FDR's braces were touched up by editors to eliminate the braces.

According to several friends of the President, an attempt was made in 1936 by an unfriendly newspaper publisher to compile a portfolio of harmful pictures, to be published before the election. According to this story, the President's friends in the White House press corps thwarted efforts by the photographer sent to do the job. This story could not be confirmed for this book.

It is believable, at least in a sense. Almost all the White House regulars liked the President and were protective of him on the matter of his legs. In fact, it went beyond that. James Roosevelt quoted photographer Sammy Schulman on why the journalists obeyed the unwritten rule. ". . . He

treated us well, so we treated him well. There was never a
public figure who was so accessible to the press, who was so
responsive to them and easy with them, who treated them
as equals and would joke with them. . . . Then you have to
remember that he arrived during Depression days and remained into the war. These were hard times and he was our
hope. To have done anything to tear him down in the eyes
of the public would have been unthinkable."

These themes run through all the memoirs and reminiscences of White House regulars of that era. "It was a
condition of the times," said Hugo Johnson. "We wanted
him to succeed."

Even those who may not have wanted him to succeed may
have felt a social restraint on reporting about his condition. Walter Trohan of the *Chicago Tribune* was no New
Dealer, but he has written that "those were quite simple
days when the press was closer to the President than ever
before or since." It was an affectionate closeness. He clearly
included himself in that romance. It was especially true at
Warm Springs. The number of "regulars" who made trips
to Georgia with the President was quite small relative to
later years. Perhaps a dozen or fewer would go south with
him. (A generation later, a traveling press corps of more
than 200 members was not unusual.) President, staff and
press saw a lot of each other in Georgia retreats. The
press gave regular parties, with skits and songs. Trohan
recalled one in which Roosevelt refused to leave, staying till
3 A.M. "drinking old fashioneds, which, as you know, is a
polite way of taking straight whiskey. At that hour, J. Russell Young of the *Washington Star* . . . had to tell him there
were times when newspapermen knew more than Presi-

dents and that moment was one, because it was time for the President to go home whether or not he wanted to."

At another such Warm Springs gathering, Roosevelt, apparently relaxed with several old-fashioneds or his favorite martinis, began spinning out the details of how Al Smith got him to run for governor in 1928. A frantic Marvin McIntyre began waving at him from behind the reporters' backs, afraid he would reveal more than he should. He didn't go too far. Probably if he had, his audience would have regarded it as off the record. At Warm Springs more than anywhere else, the professional tension between President and press was eased.

Felix Belair of the *New York Times* recalls a golf match there involving himself and George Durno of the International News Service. Belair was a fine golfer—about a four or five handicap. Durno, a favorite of Roosevelt's, was a duffer. One afternoon, Roosevelt proposed to Belair that he play Durno. Belair offered to spot Durno a stroke a hole. No, said the President, instead Belair must *throw* the ball every other stroke rather than hitting it with a club.

The next day, the match began, with Roosevelt keeping score. Belair learned quickly that throwing a golf ball for distance was hard on the arm, so he would just toss the ball a few feet underhanded on his alternate shots.

Roosevelt imposed another handicap. When in a trap, he told Belair, you must throw or hit the ball while lying flat on your back.

Roosevelt and a few other correspondents followed the pair around the nine-hole course till the match ended with Belair winning. Roosevelt laughed and joked all the way. If ever Roosevelt were guilty of false gaiety at Warm

Springs, it may have been in moments like this one. The one sport he excelled at before polio struck was golf. He had been one of the best players at the Poughkeepsie course. Roosevelt was a great teaser of journalists. Merriman Smith of the United Press was out riding a rented horse on one of the old dirt roads at Warm Springs one day when the President nearly ran him down in his little convertible. Smith reined in his horse to let the President pass. Roosevelt bowed his thanks, then "in tones that must have been audible a block away . . . hailed me with: 'Heigh-o, Silver!' " (That was in 1945. "As far as I was concerned," Smith wrote, "those were his last words.")

An example of the relaxed and friendly relationship of President and press then, and of their mutual affection for Warm Springs, is this exchange of poems. In 1943, the press association reporters heard a rumor that a long trip somewhere was in the offing. Alluding to a favorite Roosevelt topic for sniping at them—their inflated Warm Springs expense accounts—the correspondents typed up this:


Ode to the Spring
or
Expense Account, Oh, How I Miss You


As we wish for sectors vernal
Warm (like hope) Springs eternal.
There we'd bask in liquid pleasure
While piling up a modest treasure.
The problem's simple, answer same—
Let's jump to Georgia once again.

Roosevelt was handed the poem by Marvin McIntyre. He got a piece of scratch paper from Grace Tully and dashed off a reply:

> Your touching deep desire
> Arouses in me fire
> To send a hasty wire
> To Warm Springs in the mire
> To Scrape the roads
> Break out the corn
> The gals is waiting
> Sho's you born
>
> ――――――――
>
> To the 3 Press Associations
> ONLY
> None others need Apply.

That year and again in 1944, the White House Correspondents Association personally gave Roosevelt a $1,000 check for the fight against infantile paralysis. The money was raised through the association's annual dinners. In accepting the 1944 check at a regular White House press briefing (Roosevelt met with reporters twice *a week* throughout his administration), the President engaged in some brief banter, then turned serious. "That's perfectly grand," he said, "perfectly fine. Well, the dinner—the dinner was certainly worth it. It was all right." He displayed genuine emotion. He seemed genuinely moved.

Had there not been such a good relationship, perhaps there would have been occasional pictures of Roosevelt in an aide's arms, or crawling, or struggling in or out of a car, or wobbling on braces and crutches. Perhaps there would have been word descriptions of his problems.

And perhaps not. Steve Early had a set speech for newcomers. "Why write about it [or photograph him]?" he would ask. "What's the point? Everybody knows he's cripple. It's just not news." Even journalists who did not like Roosevelt would probably agree with that.

If they didn't, there was always the Secret Service. As noted above, memories differ on whether agents would actually interfere. Secret Service records dealing with the Roosevelt era are still restricted. A request to the Roosevelt Library for access to records dealing with Secret Service instructions or memoranda regarding photographers brought the response that there were no such orders or memos. So presumably, if there were censoring efforts by agents, they were either by individuals acting on their own —or the "unwritten rule" for journalists was also an unwritten rule for agents.

There is a filmstrip in the Roosevelt Library that shows the President walking with difficulty and awkwardness. The movie was taken by an amateur photographer as Roosevelt entered a reception at Vassar College in August 1933. An unidentified man, presumably a Secret Service agent, suddenly walks between the cameraman and the President. It appears his intention was to shield the President. A Maryland movie hobbyist has told the author that in 1938 he tried to take a movie of President Roosevelt as he was getting out of the car to ascend some stairs to an outdoor speaking platform. A Secret Service agent cupped his hand over the movie camera lens and kept it there till the President was in place to speak, the Maryland man said.

It should be said that Roosevelt's nearly strengthless legs posed a special problem for the Secret Service. He could not jump back, crouch or duck from a standing position. He was an especially vulnerable target for an assassin. The agents on the White House detail knew this. They also knew that Roosevelt had been shot at after he was elected but before he had taken office. Both the above incidents dealing with movie cameras, and others like them, could be explained by agents' wariness of unfamiliar persons pointing gadgets at the President.

In this regard, the Secret Service procedure in the event of a suspected assassination attempt was to shove the President down. The other big fear of the Secret Service, and *the* big fear of Roosevelt, himself, was fire. The White House of the 1930s and early 1940s was viewed by the Secret Service as "the biggest firetrap in America," in Mike Reilly's words. In the event of fire anywhere in the White House, the plan called for two agents to go immediately to the room the President was in, enter without knocking and carry him out of the building. Two canvas fire chutes were carried by the Secret Service wherever Roosevelt traveled.

A threatening crowd situation occurred once. That was in the 1940 campaign when Roosevelt came into the New York metropolitan area. Jersey City Mayor Frank ("I Am the Law") Hague, the Democratic leader of the state of New Jersey, had sent out 30,000 invitations to meet the President when he got off of the train in Newark to be wheeled to a waiting car. The station was so jammed that an alarmed Reilly asked the local police inspector if he couldn't clear people out. The reply was that Hague's invitation took the matter out of the police's hands. The people in the back who couldn't see were pushing and shoving in the small station. "The President could get killed," Reilly said. He had agents surround the wheelchair, ordered the bandleader to play the national anthem, and rushed the President to a small office during the respectful pause. Then to the car. Even in the street, the crowd was still a threat until the entourage got away from the station area.

It fell to the Secret Service to devise a number of unique artifacts because the President of the United States could not ambulate in a normal way. Ramps for all speaking engagements had to meet Secret Service specifications for strength and incline. Two speaking stands were built by the two radio broadcasting networks working with the agent in charge, E. W. Starling. One stand traveled with the President, the other went ahead to be set up on the platform.

And during World War II White House wheelchairs had gas masks as standard equipment.

Roosevelt took an embarrassing fall at the Democratic National Convention in 1936. It was held in the University of Pennsylvania's football stadium at night. He was advancing to the platform to deliver his acceptance speech, walking stiff-legged through a throng of people, on the arm of his son James, accompanied by several aides and bodyguards. He saw the elderly, white-bearded poet Edwin Markham in the crowd and waved to him. Markham thought the President wanted to shake his hand, so he reached for him. At that moment he was shoved against

James, who fell against his father. The weight of the two Roosevelts caused the right leg brace to come unsnapped. The President fell, throwing his arms up for balance, sending the loose pages of his speech scattering. Reilly caught him under the arm just before he hit the ground. Gus Gennerich snapped the brace lock in place. Roosevelt was righted, "white and worried . . . badly shaken," according to Reilly. "Clean me up," the President snapped. "Okay, let's go." Then he saw Markham, crying at the fall he caused. Roosevelt smiled, shook his hand, and walked to the stand to the cheers of 100,000 unknowing Democrats.

According to Roosevelt's physician, Admiral Ross McIntire, some reporters in the press section saw the fall. If they did, they chose to ignore it. A perusal of many news accounts of the next day produces no evidence of a fall. H. L. Mencken wrote in the *Baltimore Sun* that the President's delivery of his speech was once uncertain—a fact that was due, whether Mencken knew it or not, to the hurried and imperfect recollection of the text's pages—but other accounts missed even that.

The fact that there were so few "health" stories in the general press led to some suspicions of the Washington press corps. Leonard Fowler, editor of the *Fox Valley* (Illinois) *Mirror*, charged that there was "a conspiracy to remain mute concerning the infirmities of the President." He said the excuse was "we should not take advantage of a sick man, [but] a physical cripple is inclined to become an emotional and spiritual cripple." This charge—that Roosevelt's lameness per se was no issue but what was happening to his mind because of the polio was—was typical of the attacks that came to be made on Roosevelt. Newspapers, magazines and the broadcasting industry were not the media of this campaign, but rather specialized publications and whispers. Roosevelt was the subject of what has been called the most persistent, vicious whispering campaign in modern times.

(Fowler's point was a belief widely shared about victims of poliomyelitis at the time. It was a belief almost diametrically opposite the truth. While there were varieties of personality reactions and adjustments to being so afflicted, the large majority of polios had happy and pleasant outlooks on life. Every visitor to Warm Springs noticed that. Roosevelt's family and closest friends who wrote memoirs all made the point that he was almost never despondent after the first few months of his affliction.

Another widely believed error about polio was that it affected the mind. Dr. Kitchens asked Roosevelt to test this theory in Warm Springs once, by taking a memory test. Roosevelt could identify 24 of 25 names of the sort one learns in high school and never thinks of again.

A third mistaken notion about men who have paralysis of the sort Roosevelt had is that they are impotent. There were rumors to this effect then. James Roosevelt said in a 1976 book that his father was so affected. But the physicians who examined him for the *Liberty* article in 1931 said he wasn't. Physicians and therapists who knew Roosevelt at Warm Springs also say that he wasn't.)

Hate-gossip about Roosevelt's health had always been present, but it stayed in the background until the summer of 1935. In June of that year, Republican Senator Thomas D. Schall of Minnesota read his colleagues a business tipster sheet that said Roosevelt's "inane replies" to questions and "mental vagaries" were "beginning to fulfill our predictions." The nation appeared to be awash in such private publications. *News-Week* magazine characterized typical gossip: "The after-effect of infantile paralysis has driven the President insane! To relieve the pain of his infirmity, he had taken to drugs!! . . . The President was a hopeless, helpless invalid!!!

"Fast in pursuit chased a contradictory yarn: the President's infirmity had wholly left him; his lameness was just a fake to get the nation's sympathy."

*News-Week* made the whispering its lead article in its July 20 issue. The article was rebuttal and a rebuke. It showed a healthy Roosevelt swimming on the first page, then 11 shots of his face taken between June 1932 and July 1935. He appeared vibrant and fit. He had aged not at all. (In 1936 Anne O'Hare McCormack of the *New York Times* noted that of all the heads of state she knew, only Roosevelt had not noticeably aged during the years of the world depression.) *Time* magazine also reported that Washington correspondents "have been plagued by queries from editors and publishers back home" concerning "tales roaring through the country in whispers [that FDR] had grown mentally irresponsible." *New York Times* Washington correspondent Arthur Krock wrote a column about the rumors, concluding that the truth was Roosevelt was as mentally alert as ever, but that it was hot in Washington, some New Deal programs were being thwarted and Roosevelt was displaying "administrative and political weakness. . . . But he is still the same old Roosevelt." Stanley High of NBC broadcast that his own investigation showed the President was in no way disabled.

How had it all started? Some attributed it to a lone advertising man, E. P. Cramer of Plainfield, New Jersey. On March 28, 1935, Cramer had written a letter to C. E. Groesbeck, chairman of the Electric Bond and Share Co., suggesting some ways the utility could protect itself against "political attack" and destroy "the 'new deal' which is the motivating force behind the attack." He suggested a six-point program, most of which was simple public relations and lobbying. But point three was "A 'whispering campaign' designed to create popular suspicion that the 'new dealers' and especially the 'New Dealer-in-Chief' are either incompetent or insane." There is no evidence Groesbeck or any other executive there put the whispering campaign into motion. Nor is it likely that a single source would have gotten the results that ensued. But a Senate committee investigating lobbying called Cramer before it that August, read him some of the stories about the widespread whispering campaign and asked him if he had any "secret feeling of satisfaction." No, he said, he was ashamed of what he had done. But, he told critical senators, as if to justify himself, Democratic publicists had spread stories that Herbert Hoover was insane.

There was at least one victim of the whispering campaign. Cramer was fired by Edison Industries.

A casualty of sorts was the Washington correspondent, Richard Waldo, who wrote a "Confidential: Not for Release" article for the McClure Syndicate. The article went to 300 newspaper editors, and it said Roosevelt had been discovered at his desk in a deep coma. He was taken to sea to recuperate. A cover story had been put out that he was fishing in the Gulf of Mexico, but actually he was under guard on a Naval vessel. Since Roosevelt had been seen fishing by members of the press (he landed a tarpon the day the newsletter was issued), the rumor was easily disproved. When he returned to Washington, Roosevelt called some reporters into the Oval Office, showed them the article and told them he thought the press ought to do something about it. The National Press Club exerted pressure on Waldo, and he eventually resigned.

The summer of 1935 was not the end of the rumor-mongering at Roosevelt's expense, though it was probably the high-water mark. Stories about his health popped up again and again until his death—though increasingly these had to do with his heart, with stroke and his general state, in no way related to polio.

So, too, did stories about his role in the fight against infantile paralysis. In 1934 a committee had been formed to raise money for that fight through the device of Birthday Balls on the weekend of the Roosevelt birthday each January 30. Millions and millions of dollars were raised by that and a successor organization. Much went to Warm Springs. Eugene Talmadge told some people he thought the thing was "a racket."

William Dudley Pelley, president of Pelley Publishers and head of the Silver Shirt Legion of America, Inc., wrote an article in 1939 for *Liberation* magazine in which he charged that the fund-raising connected with the balls was political, run by "Jim Farley's boys," and that Roosevelt got the proceeds. Pelley went on and on; the article finally became a 48-page pamphlet that was sold by itself. Pelley ran a cartoon of FDR running his fingers through coins and sacks labeled "Birthday Fund." A crippled girl on crutches stood outside his window saying, "And everybody went to the birthday balls thinking they were aiding *me!*" This was referred to the Attorney General, who replied, "There seems to be no doubt that the booklet and magazine article constitute libel," but he recommended against suit since under North Carolina law (the state of publication), Pelley could print a retraction and be fined only one cent. Besides, the Attorney General said, you might even get a not-guilty verdict, on the grounds that neither publication was really widely circulated. He said federal conviction was also doubtful. Roosevelt apparently wanted something done. Steve Early suggested to Basil O'Connor that the National Foundation for Infantile Paralysis sue Pelley. Early would not have done that on his own. At any rate, the foundation decided not to do anything.

The foundation was the successor organization to the President's Birthday Balls Committee. The success of that foundation in the battle against polio was in the process of becoming one of the outstanding stories of the century in the battle against disease.

## A note on sources for this chapter

*All But the People: Franklin D. Roosevelt and His Critics 1933-1939,* by George Wolskill and John A. Hudson, has a chapter on the whispering campaigns. I also used *Merriman Smith's Book of Presidents: A White House Memoir,* edited by Tim Smith. Also, *White House Physician* by Ross T. McIntire. Some books previously cited have material dealing with the general subject covered in this chapter. The Trohan quotes are from a letter to the author. The zany golf game was described by Felix Belair in an interview. The Senate hearings dealing with lobbying and the whispering campaign at which Mr. Cramer testified were published as a government document. Details on the pool construction are in the National Archives. The *New York Daily News* for the indicated dates was used.

# Dancing for the President

---

They finally tore down the old Meriwether Inn in 1934. As Roosevelt—founder of the Georgia Warm Springs Foundation and President of the United States—told the story at numerous Thanksgiving dinners, the weight of the large number of guests—over 300—plus all that turkey and fixings, caused the dining room to sink six inches in 1932. The whole hotel sank six inches in another Roosevelt telling. His chronic fear of fire always was intensified whenever he saw that old pine structure. He feared that some day there would be a real tragedy. Many old-timers were nostalgic at the prospect of a Warm Springs without the old hotel, but not Roosevelt. He was often sentimental about the good old day—but not the Inn.

Roosevelt was relieved to see the old firetrap go—but he was concerned that with it, Warm Springs was also beginning to lose that "Warm Springs spirit." Arthur Carpenter christened that era "the low gear period" of Warm Springs' development; people connected with it noticed a special spirit, too, but could not really define it. Probably all it meant was that Warm Springs was not yet institutionalized, although that institutionalization came with growth and money. "It must never become a hospital," Roosevelt said many times. It never did, quite, but it became something a little different from the pioneering fraternity of the pre-presidential years.

Growth had been consistent from the first. The number of guests at the first Founder's Day Thanksgiving Dinner, according to Roosevelt's later count once, was "ten or twelve, the next year twenty-five, the next year fifty, one hundred and fifty and so on." On another occasion, Roosevelt estimated over 30 guests at the first dinner, 80 at the second. There was no "official" scorekeeping. On another occasion, he recalled that there had been 70 people at the first dinner.

Growth brought more changes than just the razing of Meriwether Inn. It brought, for instance, a reduced charge for a week at Warm Springs, from the earlier $42 a week to $39 a week. It also brought a patient's-aid fund, created with a few earmarked donations from Roosevelt and some other wealthy supporters of the spa, plus smaller donations from a new, small group called the "Polio Crusaders," mostly patients, former patients, their families and friends. The fund was used to help pay part, and in some cases all, of that $39 for some needy patients. The eventual goal of the fund's overseers was to create a Warm Springs in which one-third the companions paid the full cost, one-third paid half, and one-third paid nothing. Before that goal could be reached, a much more sophisticated and effective fund-raising operation replaced it. It is typical of the spirit of Warm Springs that even as institutionalization began, personal touches remained. The Patient's Aid Fund was managed with great discretion. No one knew who was getting charity and who wasn't.

Growth also brought a waiting list of some 900 to 1,000 persons needing after-care, a persistent problem with political as well as institutional overtones.

And growth brought new buildings. After the Edsel Ford pool of 1928 came the Norman Wilson Infirmary, a small building for patients with minor illnesses. That building in a way was a portent of the eventual emergence of Warm Springs as something other than a one-man show. Roosevelt was not the prime mover behind the creation of that 1930 structure. Norman Wilson was a Philadelphia companion who died shortly after he left Warm Springs. Other patients and friends raised the $40,000 for it. Then in 1933 came Georgia Hall, the handsome structure that housed the administrative offices, community dining rooms, kitchen, game rooms and reception area.

The history of Georgia Hall is interesting, since out of it grew one of the most successful charity fund-raising efforts up till then or since. According to Reverend W. G. Harry, Roosevelt told him on their first meeting in 1927 that he would like to see separate state fund-raising campaigns for Warm Springs some day. Harry recalled that Roosevelt felt his adopted state should start things with a "Georgia Hall," then New York underwrite a "New York Hall." Not every state would pay for an entire building in this scheme, but eventually, every state would provide something.

That's not exactly the way it turned out. Rather, in 1933 either Atlanta businessman Cator Woolford or Roosevelt's friend Cason Callaway came up with the idea that Georgians ought to show their support of President Roosevelt by building something at Warm Springs. Arthur Carpenter wanted it to be an administration building. Whoever had the idea, Callaway took the lead in the fund-raising. It was the first broadly cast appeal for funds, beginning about the same time as the *New York Daily News* effort for the White House pool, but seeking a much larger total. Georgia Hall, in which Roosevelt recalled the good old days in 1934 and subsequently, was conceived, underwritten and built in 1933, at a cost of $125,000.

The *value* was certainly greater than that. Callaway donated not only service in fund-raising, but money for fund-raising as well—money not included in the cost of the building. L. W. (Chip) Robert, the Atlanta builder who became a member of the Roosevelt subcabinet, did the work at cost.

In 1933, that first year of the Roosevelt presidency, it was already clear that the "key man" was going to be someone or some several people other than Roosevelt in the future. From 1927 through January 1933, there had been nine meetings of the Board of Trustees of the foundation. Roosevelt attended all but one. After his inauguration, there were three more 1933 meetings of the Board and Roosevelt attended only one. There were four meetings in 1934, of which he attended only one. Of the six meetings held after 1934 and before Roosevelt's death, he attended only one.

The key man became O'Connor, who had been the co-key man to the early survival of the place, and Keith Morgan. Morgan was the imaginative insurance man and fund-raiser who had conceived of and then put together the $560,000 "key man" life insurance policy on Roosevelt with the foundation as the beneficiary. He became chairman of the finance committee and followed up the Georgia Hall campaign first with a small Carnegie Hall benefit that raised $25,000 in the fall of 1933, then with the famous Birthday Balls.

Even before he put on the benefit, Morgan was thinking grander thoughts. He suggested to Carl Byoir, the public-relations wizard, that one of his clients could rehabilitate his image if he associated himself with raising money for the victims of polio. His image could use rehabilitation. Henry Doherty was chairman of the utilities holding company, Cities Services. He had been in and out of controversy over the years. (And in and out of hospitals. He had arthritis and had sought relief at Battle Creek sanatoria and elsewhere.) In 1933 and 1934 he was in the headlines because the Federal Trade Commission charged that he had manipulated stock in a wholly owned subsidiary of his holding company to gain a $17 million profit and because a Congressman charged that he was "the biggest tax evader in the country."

Not only would his helping Warm Springs improve his image, Morgan told Doherty after Byoir brought them together, it might even "get an old pirate like you into heaven." Doherty came down for the dedication of Georgia Hall on Thanksgiving, 1933, and began discussing what his role should be. At a brainstorming session, someone, apparently Doherty, suggested that a series of balls and parties to celebrate the President's birthday would be a good method of raising funds nationwide. He offered to make a substantial contribution toward the cost of the effort. A special committee composed of such nationally known leaders as industrialist Harvey Firestone, New York Governor Herbert Lehman, mineworkers union boss John L. Lewis and Dr. William B. Mayo and others was formed to run, or, perhaps more accurately, front for, the effort. In December it was announced that the balls would seek money to create a permanent endowment for the Georgia Warm Springs Foundation.

Amid a great publicity blitz, the balls were held on January 30, 1934. There were 6,000 of them! Roosevelt spoke on a nationwide radio hookup, not as President so much, he said, but "more as the representative on this occasion of the hundreds of thousands of crippled children in our country." He said Warm Springs could use "the generous gifts which are being made tonight [to] increase its usefulness nationally. . . . We shall be able to take more people and I hope these people will be able to come to us on the recommendation of doctors from every state in the union. . . . The fund to which you contribute tonight will undoubtedly permit us to extend the facilities of Warm Springs in a greater degree than before. . . . No man ever had a finer birthday remembrance. . . ."

The most publicized of those 6,000 balls was held at the Waldorf in New York City. It was a $25-a-ticket affair. The

President's 79-year-old mother attended. But there were also balls and other parties where much smaller donations were made. An Associated Press story said celebrations covered a spectrum from Palm Beach society to menial workers at a state hospital for the mentally ill. There were two balls in Warm Springs, one for the townspeople at a casino, the other at Georgia Hall for the patients and staff. Children in wheelchairs went through the "steps" of a country square dance.

The nation seemed caught up in a crazy mood of can-you-top-this? The world's longest telegram of congratulations was sent to the President from 40,000 Alabamans. A relay team of runners brought a short message to the White House from Baltimore. The final runner was a 57-year-old newspaper employee who worked the midnight-to-7 A.M. shift, then went out in the zero-degree cold wave that was gripping the East that week, running the 35 miles with four younger men.

(Roosevelt himself celebrated with a small group of old friends in the White House. The group had first come together in the 1920 vice-presidential campaign, and partying together on Roosevelt's birthday was a tradition.)

The money poured in. The total, after expenses of some $800,000, came to $1,016,443.59. A giant check was prepared in that amount and presented to the President for the foundation.

The question then became what to do with it. As Morgan explained later, if that money plus several hundred thousand dollars in large contributions raised by the Finance Committee in that period had been invested in 2.5 percent government securities, the foundation could have been secure for the future as it had never been before. But, he went on (in a letter to a prospective large donor in 1935), the trustees felt that "would not be true to the Foundation's ideals and its reason for existence. . . ." Therefore, it recommended another course to Roosevelt. That course the President announced to the nation on May 9, 1934, when he accepted the check.

"Let me pause here to say," Roosevelt said at the reception, "that the communications which have come to us from all parts of the country since the Birthday Ball have made it more than ever apparent that there is a shortage of properly financed orthopedic beds in many, indeed most, sections of the country. They have also indicated to us that as a result of the new interest built up by . . . a Birthday Ball, at least some of these institutions have received greater local assistance." He clearly was already thinking about the next stage of the polio fight, which would involve huge sums raised to spend not at Warm Springs but in local hospitals and in research institutions.

As to the million dollars in hand, he announced that the money would be spent in three ways. A $100,000 fund would be established "to stimulate and further the meritorious work being done in the field of infantile paralysis . . . elsewhere than at Warm Springs." A $650,000 fund "for the furtherance of the present work done at . . . Warm Springs." He said he would leave the details to the trustees but expected there would be increased interchange of doctors and therapists in Warm Springs and other communities. The remaining quarter of a million dollars would be used for the physical plant at Warm Springs.

The effort was so successful that Roosevelt decided to "donate" his birthday to the cause every year. The following November, at a morning press conference in the Little White House, Roosevelt explained the decision. It was very informal, as usual. "Drape yourselves around," he began. "Sit on the sofa, Russell [Young, a reporter]. Fred [Storm, another reporter] does not have to sit down today. . . . Well, I asked the Trustees [of the foundation] to come here today because we have been working on this thing for a couple of weeks now, on the subject of a Birthday Ball. . . . Henry L. Doherty suggested another Birthday Ball and we put it up to the Trustees and the Trustees made a recommendation. . . ."

That recommendation, in a letter to Roosevelt, which he read to the reporters, was for another ball in 1935, but this time the money would not be for Warm Springs. Seventy percent of it, he read, would be used to provide care and treatment in the community where it was raised, and 30 percent would be used for medical research to develop prevention and immunization. Then he read a letter from him to Doherty saying he agreed. Roosevelt told the reporters off the record: "I think this will be a great thing because it means that a great many communities—and this is not for quotes at all—have *no* facilities, and will now be able to start their own. . . ."

The January celebrations that followed in 1935, 1936 and 1937 were similar to the 1934 effort, but they had less than the desired results. Not as much money was raised in any year as had been in 1934. O'Connor and others suspected this was partly due to Roosevelt's increasing unpopularity with the well-to-do who could afford the larger donations, the higher-priced balls. Some others seemed to feel that the polio fight was too partisan. They lumped together the President, the President's Commission and Warm Springs. An even less desirable result of the new effort was that a research project seeking a vaccine produced one that was not only ineffective for that purpose, but resulted in a death; then another effort produced six deaths. The problem, as the scientists who later produced successful vaccines saw it, was that the effort was not focused, as it should have been, on basic research into the cause of the disease, but sought a dramatic shortcut to a way to prevent it. There were some successes, but the consensus view on the research done for the Birthday Balls Commission was that it was "a minus," as Dr. Thomas M. Rivers, the great virologist and adviser to the National Foundation for Infantile Paralysis, later put it.

The National Foundation was formed after the 1937 birthday. Roosevelt emphasized in announcing this in September of that year that the new foundation's activities would include Warm Springs only "among many others," and that "in fairness to my official responsibilities, I cannot at this time take a very active part in the much broader work that will be carried out by the new foundation, and I therefore do not feel that I should hold any official position in it." O'Connor became its president.

The new foundation soon proved to be one of the most imaginative fund-raising enterprises the world of cheerful giving had ever seen or ever would see. A letter from Keith Morgan to Grace Tully dated December 10, 1937, gives some idea:

Dear Grace:

Just off the Press and in the mails tonight!
Following is a progress report to date:

1. Donated advertising space in national magazines now totals over 30,000,000 circulation.
2. Car-cards in busses, street cars of the leading cities, coast to coast.
3. Completion of plan with telegraph companies whereby anybody can send an Infantile Paralysis greeting for 25¢ . We get the whole quarter.
4. Posters in all Pullman trains.
5. The Pennsylvania Railroad is going to use 8,500 posters in their stations; they will have subscription books in every station agent's hands; 20,000 menu tabs; bulletins on their employees bulletin boards; and a full page in their house organ called the "Mutual Magazine."
6. 1700 out of 3000 counties in the United States are now set up with County Chairmen. One county in Iowa has appointed 80 small community chairmen.
7. Organization Package #1 will be in the hands of all chairmen the middle of next week.
8. Plans are being made to extend the Pennsylvania Railroad plan to all railroads.
9. Plans are being made to extend a participation plan to all members of the American Bankers Association's Savings Banks.
10. Full participation of the motion picture industry. Warner Brothers are making two shorts. Walt

Disney is doing a Mickey Mouse on joining the fight against Infantile Paralysis. Eddie Cantor and a committee of 60 radio and screen stars are working on a MARCH OF DIMES over the radio.

11. Eddie Guest is doing a poem on Infantile Paralysis, which he will give over the air during the next two weeks.

12. The national radio program opens up on Sunday, December 12th, with a dramatization of Infantile Paralysis by the American Medical Association, and an appeal by Dr. Morris Fishbein, on the N.B.C. at 6 to 6:30 P.M., Eastern Standard Time. I go on the air on Monday, December 13th, over C.B.S. at 7:30 to 7:45 P.M., Eastern Standard Time.

A lot of other things are in the "works" and so, we roll merrily along.

Hope to see you all next week.

> With my best,
> Keith

The new organization netted over a million dollars, all of which it disbursed. In following years, half the funds were left in local communities.

The "March of Dimes" was an Eddie Cantor invention. He occasionally visited Roosevelt in Warm Springs and Washington. He says he suggested a fund-raising appeal seeking dimes to be mailed directly to the White House when the President asked him if he could "organize a million men for me who'll give a dollar a year." Thereafter, during the week before the Birthday Balls, the leading radio celebrities would make an appeal for dimes on their own programs and also get together for a special appeal program. They were highly successful. In 1939, for example, $217,602.28 was raised for the National Foundation by the March. The balls grossed about nearly $2 million that year, before expenses.

There were still political suspicions. General Hugh Johnson, the former head of the New Deal's National Recovery Administration, was chairman of the National Foundation in New York in 1939. He wrote Press Secretary Steve Early that as long as Roosevelt accepted the effort "as a personal tribute," there would be problems in raising money. He noted the irony. "It is true that the movement would never have been started in any other way, but now I am shocked to find that precisely the same consideration that started it now threatens to kill it—or at least make it difficult or impossible for it to succeed."

Roosevelt responded with a letter to Morgan a few days before the 1939 balls, to be used to counter what Johnson was seeing. He summarized the history of the fight against polio. "I should like at the same time to clarify any misunderstanding that may have arisen concerning the holding of these celebrations on my birthday. That is only an incident—and, to my way of thinking, a very important incident, too. As is the case in other campaigns on a national basis, it is usual to pick some week or day as a pivotal date around which the raising of funds may gather force and direction. . . . Politics or partisanship have, of course, played no part in any of the campaigns. . . ."

Most of the public seemed to agree. A Reg Manning cartoon of the period showed a donkey, elephant, John Q.

Public, a crippled child on crutches and FDR (standing without crutches or cane), as a file of dimes with rifles marched under banners identifying them as "Rich Men's Dimes," "Poor Men's . . . Labor, Capital, Democratic and Republican" dimes.

The dimes and the dollars began to swell. The dynamic and creative leadership of O'Connor and Morgan produced new events—such as the wartime solicitation of movie-goers for funds by ushers as they sat in the theater. Roosevelt and O'Connor discussed ending the Birthday Balls for the duration, but decided not to. The increased prosperity and patriotism that war brought also brought a great leap for the National Foundation—it grossed over $5 million in 1943—$18 million in 1945!

One idea that did much to generate donations in 1942 was the use of a "poster child." Each year thereafter, a young polio victim was chosen to symbolize the March of Dimes, Birthday Balls and other fund-raising. That first child was a four-year-old New Yorker, Gerry King, who lunched with the President at the White House, then punched movie star Dorothy Lamour in the nose when she kissed him. That episode symbolized the appeal of the National Foundation's effort—the President, the movie star, the child. To many in the field of philanthropy, this combination was unfortunate, since it drew contributions away from the diseases that affected more people. Both O'Connor and Roosevelt publicly ridiculed such criticisms.

There were other criticisms—even from Dr. Hubbard's replacement down at Warm Springs, Dr. Michael Hoke— to the effect that the publicity needed to raise the funds also raised false hopes for many polio victims. O'Connor came to be even more of a target than Roosevelt, as increasingly he became seen as the personification of grasping money-raising. Some of the attacks on him were personal. He seemed to love it. He described his transition from reluctance to enthusiasm in the job, with a quote deliberately chosen for its double meaning. He compared himself to Andrew Jackson at the Battle of New Orleans—"hip-deep in blood, and loving it."

Warm Springs, meanwhile, was continuing to grow and change. On the eve of war, it had become a relatively big endeavor, by its old standards. Its balance sheet listed a million-and-a-half-dollar balance, and it was raising and spending about a half-million dollars a year. Much of its income came from the National Foundation. Roosevelt, himself, was a consistent donor. This money was usually "found" money, unexpected income. Once he suggested an idea for a short story. Several writers took a turn at solving what was dubbed "The President's Mystery Story." *Liberty* magazine paid him $9,000 for it, which he donated to Warm Springs. When his mother died, he received many contributions for charity, all of which he sent to Warm Springs. There was an "F.D.R. Special Fund" at the spa, which was used to support needy patients. Though he seems to have let subordinates disburse it most of the time, Roosevelt could control it. Because he did on occasion direct that certain patients be helped financially, and because he did at times see to it that certain patients did not have to go on the waiting list or be treated by the admissions office in a routine fashion, there were stories about the "politics" of Warm Springs and the National Foundation. The stories greatly exaggerated what was going on.

Routinely, letters or calls to the White House from influential people about polio victims were referred to O'Connor or Keith Morgan or some other National Foundation official. And usually the response was to refer the inquirer to the National Foundation chapter in his local community. There are an estimated 3,000 letters to Roosevelt from victims or on behalf of them in the Roosevelt Library for the 1933-45 period. Most ask not for direct aid, but rather for a word of encouragement or advice. Roosevelt replied personally to around ten a month on the average until the war started. Thereafter, he personally replied to very few, but Grace Tully answered many in his behalf.

However, the war did not divert his attention from Warm Springs. In ways, it focused his attention there. In February 1941, he got a letter from Sumner Welles at the State Department suggesting that the son of the President of Paraguay be brought to Warm Springs for treatment of his polio. He said this might keep Paraguay from becoming an ally of the Axis Powers. "S.W.—Excellent—F.D.R.," Roosevelt replied. The youth came to Warm Springs. Fred Botts wrote Roosevelt that he was having trouble getting orthopedic appliances, because of the wartime shortage. Roosevelt sent a memo to his aide James Rowe to "get Warm Springs put on the priority list like all hospitals." When late in the war one of the new doctors at the hospital at Warm Springs thought he might be drafted, Roosevelt had both his physician, Admiral Ross McIntire, and his military aide, General Edwin "Pa" Watson, intervene. The doctor was reclassified. Roosevelt also put pressure on O'Connor to provide facilities at Warm Springs for servicemen, and a Navy unit was set up there.

The hospital—technically the Medical Building—had been built in 1939. It was a modern, three-story, fireproof 55-bed (later more) orthopedic surgical facility. A school and occupational-therapy building also went up in 1939, a chapel with "pews" for wheelchairs, a theater of similar design, two new dormitories for ambulatory patients, a brace shop. It was quite a campus. (During the war, a new indoor treatment pool was completed. After the war, other new structures went up, including Roosevelt Hall, a rehabilitation center and auditorium.) The Warm Springs facility's capacity grew gradually. There were 267 patients in residence during 1934, over 400 in 1941, over 500 in 1942, 700 in 1946. That's not at one time. There were never more than 122 patients there at one time during Roosevelt's lifetime.

There were staff changes. A new generation of healers came—though many of the young physiotherapists of 1927 stayed through the 1940s. Dr. Hubbard was replaced by Dr. Michael Hoke, an Atlanta orthopedic surgeon. "He made it an *orthopedic* center," Carpenter believed. As the demands grew, Hoke got an assistant, Dr. C. E. Irwin, another orthopedic surgeon—and a brilliant one—who was then at Emory University Medical School in Atlanta. He succeeded Hoke later in the 1930s. By the end of that decade, the medical staff consisted of a chief surgeon (Irwin), his assistant (Dr. Stuart Raper), a "general physician" (J. A. Johnson), Alice Plastridge as superintendent of physical therapy, plus a number of other professional people, including a corsetiere.

Carpenter had never been able to work well with O'Connor, who remained treasurer of the Warm Springs Foundation. Carpenter left, to be replaced by Louis Haughey. Botts, uncomfortable with the growing institutionalization, tried to resign, but was talked out of it by Roosevelt. Roosevelt was often nostalgic about the good old days. He saw Carpenter in 1939, after the latter had left the Warm Springs Foundation. They reminisced. Carpenter got the impression Roosevelt objected to the inevitable progress. Henry Toombs, Roosevelt's friend and the architect who designed so many of the buildings in Warm Springs, noticed that Roosevelt always preferred the old pools to the new one built up the hill in 1942. He thought that was partly due to the growing need for privacy, partly due to the fact that Roosevelt liked to remember the early days swimming alone in the old pool, looking up at the pines around it.

Also, Roosevelt had an attachment for the old pool, since he had had a hand in designing its bathhouse. Toombs sent him his plans, and got back a detailed memo and sketch calling for changes. Later when Toombs designed a residence hall, Roosevelt asked for detailed changes. "Take out linen closets between wards and restore passageway . . . put hand basin in bath room. . . . Put door from West Ward into Chart Room. . . . Dark Room can be made smaller. . . . X-ray room smaller and lab larger . . . toilet next to Waiting Room should enter from Waiting Room & *not* from Dr. Hubbard's office. . . . No connection from lower kitchen & upper . . . nurse's bedroom taken out of Photograph room and connect to toilet . . . no indoor stair. Why not put outside stair in middle of porch and let it come into middle hallway of basement. . . ." All this hastily scrawled on official stationery in the Governor's Mansion in Albany.

Roosevelt's interest in architecture remained keen, but he had less impact on Warm Springs buildings after he became President. For one thing, Toombs and Arthur Carpenter conspired against him. When Georgia Hall's preliminary plans were drawn, Roosevelt asked to see them. The architect and the business manager sent him instead a simple sketch, "having agreed between ourselves that if we showed him the detail drawings he would surely be full of ideas and probably upset our plans, which were already far along," Toombs wrote later. "We had noted that whenever F.D.R. saw a drawing he always reached for a pencil."

Roosevelt "reached for a pencil" a lot. He and Henry Pope conceived the master plan for Warm Springs development in 1926 and 1927. Roosevelt wrote Toombs in the latter year that he favored "[no] formal location of buildings . . . in other words a sort of haphazard spacing of the buildings in proper relation to the trees on the three different hill slopes." He had already by then designed his own first home in Warm Springs, with Toombs doing the drawings and supervising the construction. It was a very simple frame house, based on a typical "Southern Greek Revival" home Roosevelt had seen in a nearby town. He suggested to Toombs that its interior take the typical "dog trot central hall" and widen it so that it could serve as a dining-room-living room combination. The house cost just over $7,200. Roosevelt hoped he was setting a pattern of simplicity and economy for others to follow. He himself followed it. In 1932 he had Toombs do another house for him that came to be called "the Little White House," and also came to be a part of history. The cost was $7,350 for it and a garage. The example influenced some Warm Springs colonists and did not influence others. Arthur Carpenter had Toombs do him a $12,000 house there in 1934. Of course, that was a year-round home, not a cottage. Keith Morgan's cottage cost $6,500. Lynn Pierson's Toombs-designed cottage cost $45,600 in 1935.

The Little White House was based on a house Roosevelt had seen in the nearby town of Greenville. He was a strong believer in copying local styles. He persuaded his mother to build a small cottage to rent to patients and families of patients. He persuaded Toombs to design it in the style of an old Meriwether Inn servant cabin. The Little White House was located at the brow of a hill, on the very edge of a ravine. Roosevelt wanted a sun porch overlooking the ravine, where he would work (often at a card table) in nice weather. The simplicity of what came to be on occasion the headquarters of the United States government is suggested by the fact that when he wanted to work indoors in chilly weather, he had the card table moved in in front of the fireplace.

The frame house with dark stained pine interiors (no plaster, FDR ordered) has a kitchen and pantry, two small bedrooms connected by a bathroom, and a room and bath off the porch for a secretary, and the living-dining combination. It was furnished mostly with items from the first Roosevelt cottage, including furniture made at a small factory at Val-Kill, one of Eleanor's enterprises in Dutchess County. There were ship models and nautical prints; a ship's lantern on the front porch was always lit when the President was in residence. The porch was colonnaded, as the Southern Greek Revival style required. It must have been galling to Roosevelt, who felt so strongly about the

South's becoming self-sufficient, that Toombs had to order the columns from Chicago. Roosevelt had urged Toombs to use "local woods" for paneling, even when it was expensive. He told him to make up for it by installing the "cheapest possible fixtures." Roosevelt knew of this and other details of the project because he demanded and received weekly reports from the construction superintendent on material used, the number of men employed, the weather, the progress of the work. That was during the fall and winter of 1931-32, the period in which he was also governing New York State and seeking the presidential nomination. He and Eleanor came down in May and stayed in the Little White House for the first time. "Dear Henry," he wrote on May 5, "We are all settled in the cottage and I can't find words to tell you how delighted I am with it. So far there is nothing I want changed." But there was. He wrote J. W. Ewing of the Warm Springs Construction Co. that he wanted a flat rock mantel instead of the original wooden one, and he had a shower put in the basement for the servants. The servants' quarters were located in the garage, which had no hot water.

Over the presidential years, there were some changes— a guest house, a guard house, security arrangements—but simplicity remained the hallmark of the Little White House. It was never gilded. Toombs, who had proposed in his original plans an octagonal reception room—his client was after all Governor of New York—and who had been turned down by his client who thought this pretentious, later wrote, ". . . love of simple surroundings—a bright fire, always a cluttered room of books, papers, a few ship models, odds and ends, sometimes a curious but seldom a really fine thing formed the unstudied background in which he liked to live. I cannot imagine either him or Mrs. Roosevelt employing a decorator to 'do' a room or house for them. They would use what they had, add without much bother other necessaries. The results were homelike, personal, unpretending, livable. They were never accomplished decor, but they were honest."

It was a *comfortable* house, and for Franklin but not for Eleanor, that word also describes the social environment Warm Springs had become. In the presidential years of his life, when his hopes for his health's recovery were gone, when the press of business and responsibility were greatest and ever increasing, Warm Springs became the place Roosevelt could relax best. He could laugh everywhere, but he seems to have been able to laugh most there.

## A note on sources for this chapter

In addition to sources already cited (particularly Turnley Walker's book), the following were used: *The Gentle Legions* by Richard Carter, *Take My Life* by Eddie Cantor with Jane Kesner Ardmore, *Tom Rivers: Reflections on a Life in Medicine and Science* by Saul Benison, *The Sweeping Wind* by Paul de Kruif, and the *Souvenir Tour Guide to Franklin D. Roosevelt's Little White House and Museum.*

# *"I Didn't Do One Damn Thing"*

The housewarming for the Little White House was on May 1, a day after FDR arrived for a four-week vacation. Unlike most of the subsequent Little White House parties, it included a mixture of guest-types—politicians and businessmen from the town and county, staff members from the Georgia Warm Springs Foundation, some patients and/or relatives of patients. Another difference between the housewarming and more typical parties was that a large number of people were invited. Through the presidential years, the guest list was more often smaller; and the guests were more often just neighbors, or just hospital people, or just press and staff. Mrs. Roosevelt was there at the housewarming. She came infrequently thereafter. She was uncomfortable with the Georgians and they with her. "She always made us feel like we were under inspection," a frequenter of the parties recalled later. "He was *fun*, but she. . ." and her voice trailed off. A man who attended many of the parties at which both Roosevelts were present recalled that once he took her arm to lead her to the dinner table, in what he thought was the properly gallant southern style, and she rebuked him.

After Roosevelt became President, according to the calculations of Paul Rogers, the number of parties when he was in residence increased. One reason for that was Warm Springs had become principally a place for him to relax and his principal place of relaxation. He insisted on parties. When White House staff began making preparations for a trip south, Missy LeHand or Grace Tully or someone would be instructed to make advance arrangements for the socializing as well as the other housekeeping details. That continued straight through till his death. Here is a typical letter written by Grace Tully to Louis Haughey at the foundation in 1943:

April 7, 1943

Dear Louis:

Completely "off the record", the President expects to arrive at Warm Springs, by motor, about 5:30 on Thursday, April fifteenth. I believe he plans to have dinner that evening with the patients, but you need not bother about accommodations for him or any of the party as everyone is remaining on the train that night. The next day he probably will drive around a bit and have a picnic lunch at Dowdell's Knob and will leave that evening.

He doesn't want his cottage opened up, but he would like to have the water turned on in case he wishes to go up there for an hour or so.

On the sixteenth, he would like you and Muriel, Dr. Ed and Mabel, Dr. and Mrs. Raper, and Kitty and Livy to join him for a picnic lunch.

I look forward to seeing you all then. My best to everyone.

Always sincerely,
Grace Tully

Muriel was Mrs. Haughey, Ed and Mabel were the Irwins (the chief surgeon), Dr. Raper was the assistant surgeon. Mrs. Raper was a physiotherapist. Kitty and Livy were the Livingston Fryers. She was a polio.

Another reason why the social life of Warm Springs became more active after Roosevelt was elected President, according to Rogers, was that the visitors—White House staff, press—liked so much to mix work and play. Another reason was that the permanent and semipermanent residents at the foundation had just come to know each other so well that they fell into partying more easily.

There were some 20 cottages owned by patients or their families by the early years of the Roosevelt presidency. Most of these families were well-to-do, extremely so in some cases. They set the tone of much of the social life. The Fryers mentioned in the letter epitomized this group. They were upstate New Yorkers who built a home they used just for winters. They had a butler, chauffeur and maid, all of whom spoke French. The butler wore tails. George Peabody had a cottage at Warm Springs, "Pine Glade," a 3,000-square-foot house that would have been a showplace in many resort communities. There were several others.

The foundation stopped selling lots for homesites in the mid-1930s and began buying back the homes of some of the wealthy colonists in the late 1930s, so this aristocratic segment of the population stopped dominating social life as the years rolled on.

The rich at Warm Springs were different from the rich elsewhere in the 1930s. They liked "that man in the White House." At least almost all of them did. There was one family of "Roosevelt-haters," according to the memories.

Roosevelt was, of course, at home with the upper crust. He was one of them. His party language among other things reminded his fellow revelers that he was a son of Eastern Seaboard wealth. "Infra dig" was a favorite phrase of his. He liked to ask or offer "a ciggy." But he was never pompous. And he made it difficult for his aristocratic friends to be pompous, too. Once while he was President, he drove to the home of a wealthy neighbor and honked his horn. A maid came to the door. "Is Will home?" he asked.

"Mr. Moore is not at home," she replied in a crisp French accent. "Whom shall I say called, please?"

"Tell him that Frank stopped by to say hello," he laughed and drove off.

Roosevelt probably did not have favorites at Warm Springs, but if he did, one would certainly have been Mary L. Lord, nicknamed "Sissy." In 1934, J. Cooper Lord, an old school- and clubmate, wrote Roosevelt a "Dear Frank" letter saying that his daughter Sissy had polio. Roosevelt saw to it that she got into Warm Springs. She became a regular there thereafter. The Lords built a cottage at Warm Springs, "Pine Needles." She and the President exchanged messages frequently. "It is so sad to see you go," she wrote him after his spring visit in 1938, "but we'll be seeing you again in November, and perhaps by then I will be able to dance a jig for you!" That was the Warm Springs Spirit talking, and Warm Springs magic working. She had been quite ill. When Lord first wrote Roosevelt, she was in an iron lung, and he had replied, "Ordinarily we have found it best not to take children so afflicted." Later she had spent a lot of time in a special orthopedic frame. But she kept improving. When her father died in 1939, she wrote the President, "Dear Uncle Franklin," and he signed his letters to her that way after that.

One of the few "Gold Coasters," as the very well-to-do early colonists were called, who was still in Warm Springs along with the Fryers during the war years was Mrs. Lynn Pierson, whose family had attracted the Ford donation and had provided much assistance themselves. Roosevelt called on her on his next to last visit to Warm Springs in 1944.

Another wealthy tone-setter who stayed till the end was Leighton McCarthy. McCarthy was a wealthy Canadian corporation lawyer and financier. His 15-year-old son John came down with polio in 1928. John met Roosevelt at Warm Springs, introduced his father to him. The two men became friends, there and in Washington. In Warm Springs the McCarthys bought a cottage and Leighton became an important member of the foundation's board as well as a member of the social set. In Washington he saw Roosevelt in his new role of Canadian Ambassador. He came down with Roosevelt for the last visit in 1945.

This was not the only ambience Roosevelt relaxed in while in Warm Springs. But the well-to-do were an important part of the relaxing environment Georgia provided.

As a true small-d democrat, Roosevelt enjoyed his own caste as much as others.

Politics was usually avoided in Warm Springs. After he got to be President—after he got to be Governor, probably—there was never a day in Georgia when he didn't have to devote some hours to thoughts of government and statecraft, but he tried to keep it to a minimum. That was true even when the parties brought together a lot of political figures. One oft-told Warm Springs anecdote is about the time a government official started talking business with Roosevelt and the President shut him up by bursting into song with Fred Botts.

One famous party took place at the rustic log cabin house belonging to Cason Callaway. The Callaway cabin was as elegant as it was rustic, situated in the midst of a forest, near a spring so deep that it was a startling, unbelievable royal blue. One night in the mid 1930s, a small caravan of autos drove up the winding dirt road to the cabin to discharge the President of the United States. He was without his braces, so Gus Gennerich carried him in in his arms. Inside, Gus carried the President up one flight of stairs to a maple-paneled bar, furnished with overstuffed chairs and sofas. There the party began. With Roosevelt had come Grace Tully, Marvin McIntyre, Admiral McIntire and James Roosevelt. The Callaways had invited a few wealthy friends and relatives—Mr. and Mrs. Clark Howell, he the publisher of the *Atlanta Constitution* and a long-time supporter of Roosevelt politically; Mr. and Mrs. Charles Rawson, Virginia Callaway's sister and brother-in-law; Mr. and Mrs. Hollis Lanier, her cousins; Cason's mother; a few other area dignitaries; and a surprise guest, Gay Shepperson, who was overseeing the Pine Mountain Valley experiment.

There was some initial concern that inviting her might tilt the party, since she was an outspoken New Dealer (more so than the President in Georgia), and some of the wealthy friends and relatives of the Callaways were, like many of their class, opposed to the New Deal. "But she turned out to be the life of the party," Mrs. Callaway recalled years later, as she refreshed her memory of the event with pictures taken that night.

After drinks in the bar, the party moved downstairs for dinner—charcoal-broiled mallard duck. Callaway thought mallards could become a "cash crop" for Georgians and was experimenting with them. The dinner was banquet-style, but with benches rather than chairs around the single long table in the 50-foot-long central room of the cabin. There were fires blazing in stone fireplaces at either end. After dinner, the table and benches were moved back to the sides of the room. Graham Jackson, a black pianist and accordionist from Atlanta, entertained with a group of singers dressed like old plantation workers in overalls or long calico dresses, and sunbonnets or bandannas. Callaway often had Jackson's group down to entertain Roosevelt. The first time Roosevelt heard them, he complimented them to Virginia Callaway. "Yes, we have good singers around here," she replied. "Those singers don't work for Cason; you can't fool me," he said. "Oh, yes. You know Cason won't hire one [as field hand or domestic] unless he can sing." It became a standing joke when the time came at parties for "listening to the darkies sing," as Callaway put it.

After the broiled mallard and the choir, the guests sang popular tunes of the day and some old standards to the accompaniment of the accordion. Then the table and benches were moved to one side of the room for ballroom dancing. Roosevelt sat that out, of course, with the females there taking turns sitting a dance out with him. As the evening rolled on, the revelers became more boisterous. It ended with them sliding down fire-escape chutes from the upper level to the yard, over and over again in follow-the-leader fashion. The President sat that out, too. Mrs. Callaway and others who attended such parties over the years say they never saw him indicate any frustration or sense of self-pity at being unable to join in all the frivolity. "He didn't make people self-conscious," one said. "Never."

An interesting thing to note about the friendship of Callaway and Roosevelt is that the former supported the latter politically. It went beyond their both being Democrats. Almost everybody was a Democrat in Georgia in those days, even the wealthy men like Callaway who in any northern state would almost surely have been Republican. Georgia was a one-party state at the time. (When he was informed in 1942 that a prominent Republican had been named to an Office of Price Administration post in Atlanta, Roosevelt dashed off a note to McIntyre: "Tell [Leon] Henderson [head of the OPA] this . . . has absolutely no rhyme or reason. It is literally true that in Georgia no respectable person is a Republican." Callaway not only always voted for Roosevelt, he even went so far as to let lapse his membership in the United States Chamber of Commerce, due to its fierce opposition to the President. He was that loyal. He always referred to Roosevelt in correspondence with other Roosevelt allies and aides as "the Chief." Roosevelt almost became his chief literally. When he was elected President, he offered Callaway the job of Secretary of the Navy. It would have been quite a plum for a man just 38 years old, but Callaway turned it down.

Many Georgians recall the Callaway of those days as a man who would speak out for Roosevelt or remain silent when New Deal policies—and particularly personalities— came up at the Capital City Club in Atlanta and other places that wealthy anti-Rooseveltians gathered.

Even when his mills were engaged in a bitter strike with the textile union trying to organize the South, a fight that found Roosevelt and him on opposite sides of the fence, their friendship remained. They visited each other in Georgia or the White House, and corresponded frequently. That strike tested them. Roosevelt made several speeches and other public statements condemning wages in the textile industry. He complained to a conference of newspaper editors about the way union organizers were harassed by the mill operators. Callaway, for his part, fired strikers. (Gay Shepperson hired some.) According to some union officials, this 1935 strike or one in 1934 involving other plants in Georgia, but not Callaway's, was called off after Roosevelt's private assurance that there would be no retaliation. Roosevelt did publicly urge strikers to return to work in 1934 and publicly urged firms to take them back without prejudice. Callaway wrote Roosevelt a letter explaining why the strike was unnecessary from his point of view. But except for that letter, which Roosevelt apparently did not answer, such talk about issues on which they disagreed was rare between the two. Mrs. Callaway said later she *never* heard them argue about such issues.

In connection with the textile industry, Roosevelt cer-

tainly felt on the other side of the line from the mill owners. Even those he thought were somewhat enlightened. He
told a conference of newspaper editors once that he knew of
"a certain cotton mill in the South" where wages and housing and working conditions were "good, above average,"
but that when union organizers showed up, they got "the
worst beating up that any two people could get without
getting killed." A textile worker in North Carolina once
told a Charlotte newspaper reporter that "Roosevelt is the
only man we had in the White House who would understand that my boss is a son of a bitch." That was true, no
doubt, but there is no evidence to suggest that Roosevelt
felt that way about Callaway—or cared if he was or not.

Two men who worked for Roosevelt in the period and
often went to Georgia concluded later that what was really
central to the relationship was Callaway's eagerness to be
close to power. One tells a story about how angry Callaway
became when Roosevelt did not accompany some White
House aides to a social event at his home. A researcher who
has studied the Callaway-Roosevelt correspondence concluded, "My impression—a rich man that uses his position
to seek favors from FDR & enjoy contact with high officials. Not exactly the simple farmer sharing a common interest in farm problems with FDR."

Undoubtedly, both appraisals have something to them,
but there is no denying that the two men did share a common interest in Georgia agriculture, did have imaginative
ideas about it and, most importantly, were able to relax
from hectic careers in each other's company. Callaway once
defended his friendship with words to this effect: "I know
Roosevelt liked me, else he wouldn't have been so kind and

thoughtful and considerate." Roosevelt could display that in small, memorable ways. The Callaways were once guests overnight at the White House for a white-tie dinner for the Supreme Court justices. Callaway forgot to pack his white buttons. He had the valet ask Roosevelt for a spare set. Roosevelt replied he had only one set. So an embarrassed Callaway went to the reception with black buttons. His embarrassment left him when he saw one other guest similarly improperly accessoried—the President of the United States.

Parties similar to but much smaller than the one at Blue Springs were held on a regular basis on the foundation's campus when the President was at his second home. A favorite party site was the home of the Irwins near the medical building. Often there would be only six or eight at the dinner table—the hosts, the President, Grace Tully, Steve Early, Sissy Lord, Leighton McCarthy and Fred Botts at one party recalled by Ann Irwin Bray. She was a pre-teen then, and observed the goings-on from the periphery, where she was in charge of another guest, Fala, the President's Scottish terrier. To these parties Roosevelt always came in his wheelchair. He would dominate the evening. He almost always insisted on mixing the drinks. He preferred martinis ("four to one," he told Merriman Smith, the United Press reporter) according to most of the evidence, and this may have been in large part due to the fact that he could be more theatrical in the preparation of those than other cocktails. He also served them often at the White House and the Little White House, though Hoke Shipp of the foundation staff, who was in charge of supplying the Little White House, says gin was not a noticeably big-demand item on

the drink list. He says Roosevelt liked the wine of the countryside, so to speak, and kept local fruit brandies and
moonshine along with popular brands of bourbon and
scotch on hand for himself and his guests. Moonshine was
illegal even after Repeal. It was unaged corn whisky made
in hidden spots along the Flint River. One such still was
forever after referred to as "Roosevelt's still," because, according to legend at least, he occasionally drove there with
a Secret Service agent to chat and pick up the supplies for
a party. This criminal behavior, if it did indeed occur, was
not routine procedure for stocking the liquor cabinet at
the Little White House. More often, the illicit corn was
brought over by a friend like Henry Toombs, who preferred it to commercial liquor, as did many Georgians.
This traffic was also criminal, technically, but the county
sheriff was not feared, since he was an occasional supplier
to the President, himself. Or so the local historians believe.

Sometimes the partying at Warm Springs was sequential.
It might start early, at the end of the workday, with cocktails only at the Little White House, where Roosevelt,
whatever the drink of the evening, was a real pusher. ("How
about another little sippy," he would urge friends as he
wheeled among them.) This was the portable institution
called "the Children's Hour" in Warm Springs, Washington and elsewhere. Some or all of the group would then
drive the few minutes down the mountain to the Irwins
for dinner, singing and listening to Roosevelt's corny jokes.
Mabel Irwin set down her memories of one such evening.
Harry Hopkins, head of the Works Project Administration, was there. Roosevelt kidded him in the current vein

of WPA critics, who insisted that WPA employees did not work for their pay.

"Harry, did you hear about the accident in Greenville today?"

"No, sir, Mr. President, I haven't heard. What happened?"

"Well, one of the WPA workers digging a ditch leaned on his shovel so long that the termites ate the handle out and he fell and broke his back." His face would light up at this and other corny jokes—or anything meant to lighten the night—the smile would flash, back would go his head in that exaggerated gesture of mirth, and he would roar, "I love it! Don't you just love it!" (But Roosevelt implored Eddie Cantor on another occasion to quit making WPA jokes on his radio show. He said the jobs were desperately needed by the victims of depression.)

After dinner at the Irwins, there would be singing by Botts, who had once aspired to a career in grand opera, or group singing, almost always including "Home on the Range," which was popularly and incorrectly supposed to be Roosevelt's favorite. Wherever he visited, he was greeted by it. Among friends he would express his feelings—"Oh, my Gawd!"—as the familiar first notes were hit. The party broke up again, with some guests going to a party at Cottage 13, where the female members of the White House traveling staff were quartered, or to the cottage where the press made its headquarters, or to someone else's home for further revelry well into the evening. Sometimes journalists would turn their writing abilities to fun, and the early morning hours would include skits and song parodies of somewhat more originality than the President's WPA joke. Even when he was busy at Warm Springs, he was recharging his batteries. He was relaxing. When he would go back to Washington, it was the rest and the fun that he remembered, not the work. On March 30, 1937, he chatted with reporters at a White House press conference after a visit to Warm Springs. In 14 days there he had made a nationwide radio address, hosted the Prime Minister of Canada, visited a new community house in the village (named after his mother), dedicated a school (named after his wife), made other speeches, followed closely the fight in Congress over his Supreme Court plan and conducted other business. But he recalled none of that. "That was a grand party down there this year," he said to the reporters who had traveled south with him. "It was a real holiday. It was the best holiday I ever had at Warm Springs because I didn't do one damn thing."

Warm Springs not only introduced Roosevelt to moonshine, it also introduced him to pork barbecue, Brunswick stew, fried chicken—the staples of the larger get-togethers in the South. A typical such luncheon for Roosevelt and fifty local citizens was held at the Civilian Conservation Corps camp near Warm Springs on that March 1937 visit. Dr. and Mrs. Neal Kitchens were the hosts. The local paper observed: "The barbecue was most enjoyable, perhaps by reason of its simplicity and lack of formality as any other cause. Matter of fact conversation passed between the President and his friends, just as if he were merely a common neighbor of all."

Roosevelt apparently liked Brunswick stew, usually a dish of one or two such meats as chicken, squirrel, veal, pork, plus corn and beans or onions in a very thick tomato sauce. He apparently did not like the Georgia version of barbecue, pork cooked over an open smoky fire and basted frequently in a vinegary, spicy tomato sauce. His own cook at the Little White House was Daisy Bonner, a Georgian who worked for the Peabodys and then the Irwins when the President wasn't in Warm Springs. She knew simple country Georgia fare and also the more sophisticated dishes her employers liked. Roosevelt got to like cornbread and turnip greens. Roosevelt's favorite Georgian recipe was her version of Country Captain, a chicken dish. He told everybody, falsely, that her recipe was a secret, with 45 ingredients, which was a joke between Roosevelt and Daisy.

Roosevelt introduced one new dining style to Georgia. That was the elaborate picnic. In Georgia before he came, a picnic was always the simplest sort of endeavor. Ham sandwiches, beer or soft drinks or a pitcher of tea, of lemonade, maybe cold fried chicken. Informal attire and picnic blankets instead of table and chairs. Roosevelt preferred regular dinner dishes, tables with linen, chairs or, as often as not, the back seats of his cars removed and placed on the ground. He thought picnics should be catered, that there should be servants. In addition to beer or Coke from a bottle, he had glasses and the ingredients for cocktails and a cocktail shaker along. There were several spots in the area that he preferred—"the wolf's den," a spot by a waterfall on or near his farm, reached from the Columbus Highway; "sunshine shack," a lean-to in an open field on the road from Warm Springs to Pine Mountain; the Ninth Hole at the golf course offered a picnic site; and there was Dowdell's Knob, which got a bona fide state-built spur built to it in 1937 to replace Roosevelt's own earlier effort. It thus became more suitable for large groups. (At Roosevelt's suggestion, the Georgia Highway Department built a loop at the end of the road. The President said he found the dead-end at the point where the mountain sloped down to the valley dangerous.)

The 1943 picnic was at the Knob. It was a typical Roose-veltian elegance catered by the B&O Railroad, with one wartime-inspired difference. Soldiers from Fort Benning, in battle dress, with loaded rifles and sidearms, stood along the mile-long spur, prowled the woods along either side, and guarded the celebrants from the perimeter of the cleared area at the loop.

The people of Meriwether County understood the reasoning behind such precautions—there was a permanent Marine detachment near the Little White House—but most probably considered them unnecessary. If there was one place where Roosevelt was most safe, if there was one place where harm was least likely to befall him, it was, they were sure, his beloved Warm Springs.

### A note on sources for this chapter

In addition to published material previously cited, and some of the Tugwell interviews at the Roosevelt Library, this chapter is based on interviews conducted in Georgia by the author in 1976 and 1977, on interviews conducted by Columbia Broadcasting System reporters for a 1965 television program, on brief reminiscences written shortly after Roosevelt's death by members of the Irwin family. Also, the book *Cason Callaway of Blue Springs* by Paul Schubert was useful.

# Going Home

The fatal harm that did come to Franklin Roosevelt at Warm Springs is a familiar story now. He came down by train on March 30, 1945, looking almost as bad to his friends as he had looked when he came after the harrowing election campaign the previous fall. The hard Washington winter and his advancing physical deterioration had left their mark. The train pulled into a station crowded with welcomers as usual. He descended to the ground via a small elevator—the courageous walks down the special ramps had long since been abandoned. Mike Reilly wheeled him to his blue Ford convertible and, with the aid of another agent, lifted him into the passenger seat. An agent drove him at the head of a small caravan onto the foundation's grounds, past Georgia Hall and up to the Little White House. Patients and staff were on the porch and in front of it at Georgia Hall. Not even the Thanksgiving Day dinners were a more honored tradition than the Georgia Hall welcome and the Georgia Hall farewell. Roosevelt always came by there and waved or spoke when he arrived, always paused there to say goodbye when he left.

"Total rest" was the recommendation of Dr. Bruenn, who accompanied him to Georgia. This was to be a recuperating trip. Social life was going to be at a minimum, Roosevelt's staff told his old friends. He also avoided the pool. He spent his nonworking hours (which were at first most of his waking hours) chatting with his cousins, Laura Delano and Margaret Suckley, who had become his frequent companions at Warm Springs and Hyde Park, and being driven with them about the countryside. They made several trips to Dowdell's Knob. There they just sat and looked at the signs of spring in the valley.

He went to Easter services with them at the Warm Springs Chapel on April 1, allowing himself to be lifted from his wheelchair to sit in a regular pew, a custom he had always preferred. His paleness was emphasized by the white floral decorations, the soft light, his gray suit. He participated in the songs, responsive readings and prayers—gesturing with his head as the other polios did when the able-bodied in the audience knelt. For the first time some of his Warm Springs friends noticed a constant tremor in his hands. He dropped his prayer book once, his glasses another time. Not once during the services did he smile.

On Monday, April 9, Mrs. Rutherfurd arrived for a visit. She brought Elizabeth Shoumatoff with her, to do a water-color portrait of the President. By then Roosevelt was a much different man from the gray wreck who had slumped in his convertible ten days before. Warm Springs was producing the desired effect. "The weather," Dr. Bruenn wrote, "was ideal, and . . . there was a decided improvement in his appearance and sense of well being. He had begun to eat with appetite, rested beautifully, and was in excellent spirits." Daisy was making him oatmeal gruel as a between-meals snack. At mealtimes he was soon asking for second helpings. His afternoon drives in the open car under the hot Georgia spring sun brought color back to his face.

The "magic" his second home had worked in December was obviously working again. He began to do a little work —preparing a speech, going over state papers—and made plans for more socializing. He agreed to attend as the guest of honor a late-afternoon barbecue to be given by the new Mayor Frank Allcorn, a relative newcomer from Atlanta who owned the Hotel Warm Springs in town, and the hotel manager, Ruth Stevens, a lifelong resident who had witnessed Roosevelt's first arrival over two decades before. The President planned to "eat and run." He had a date an hour later at the Playhouse at the foundation to watch the dress rehearsal of a minstrel show some of the young patients were preparing. It would be a busy social day—like the Warm Springs of old.

Roosevelt slept late on the 12th, and though he complained to Dr. Bruenn that he woke with a headache, he looked well to his doctor and his guests. He worked at his card table, wearing his Naval cape, while the artist sketched. His cousins bustled about. Mrs. Rutherfurd sat quietly in front of him. They planned a light lunch, since all were going to the barbecue. Suddenly, Roosevelt put his hand to his forehead and said, "I have a terrific headache." Then he slumped unconscious. A valet and messboy carried him the few steps into his bedroom. Dr. Bruenn was called and arrived within 15 minutes. He quickly diagnosed a massive cerebral hemorrhage. He ministered to Roosevelt for two hours. At 3:35 P.M., on a narrow single bed in a simple pine-paneled room 12 feet wide and 14 feet long, Roosevelt died. A grief-stricken Daisy Bonner entered her name and that moment into history, writing in pencil on the pantry doorjamb over the stove, "Daisy Bonner cooked the first meal and the last one in this cottage for the President Roosevelt."

Mrs. Roosevelt came down to take his body to Hyde Park. Many people in Warm Springs believed Roosevelt had decided to retire to his "second home." Others believed his declining health would at least make him a permanent winter resident in Georgia. The former is not true and the latter is doubtful. (It could get bitter on Pine Mountain in January and February.) There is no denying how much Warm Springs meant to him, in every way, but he had always been a sojourner. Graham Jackson, who had played for him at parties so often over the years, and who was scheduled to play at the minstrel show rehearsal, knew that instinctively. He was among the dozens of people who gathered in front of Georgia Hall on April 13 to watch the funeral procession take the President's body to the train station. Military bands played dirges, and battle-dress troops from Fort Benning followed them in the sad procession down the hill. Other soldiers lined the roadways. The casket was covered with the flag hastily pulled down from the flagpole at the Little White House. At Georgia Hall, on Mrs. Roosevelt's orders, the hearse stopped, keeping the tradition of farewell alive to the end. The quiet of the hot Georgia morning had been broken till then only by the soft tramp of boots, muffled drums and dirges. Now audible crying and loud groans came from the porch of the Hall. Jackson stepped forward. He was a Coast Guard recruiter, and he had on his uniform. Tears streaked his face. He played the soft sad strains of Dvorak's "Going Home" on his accordion as the procession resumed its pace.

They held Founder's Day as usual in 1945. There was a lot to be thankful for. The great war was over. The effort to end the scourge of polio had more money at its disposal —by the millions of dollars—than ever before. The Georgia Warm Springs Foundation was in good financial shape (in large part due to the $560,000 it received from the insurance companies on the death of Roosevelt; his death produced other immediately noticed profit—for example, $6,000 in royalties from Pocket Books for *Franklin Delano Roosevelt, a Memorial*). But it was a sad affair. They left an empty chair at the head table, and the patients and staff all said silent prayers with that chair in mind.

Ten years later, the National Foundation announced that field trials of the Salk polio vaccine developed in foundation-sponsored research had proved that the disease could be prevented. The announcement came on April 12. It was widely assumed that this date was chosen because of its anniversary significance. It was just the sort of thing O'Connor would do, in the view of his many critics. In fact, this was a coincidence, according to the respected scientists in charge of evaluating the tests and making that evaluation public. But what if the announcement had been contrived? The virologist Tom Rivers put it nicely: "There could be no quarrel with such a decision. What if the report had been delayed three or four days? President Roosevelt had been the founder of the National Foundation; Mr. O'Connor had been one of his closest friends—hell, they started everything—without them there would have been no Foundation, and I dare say, no vaccine. Why shouldn't the report be given on that day? It was fitting."

## *A note on sources for this chapter*

In addition to previously cited material, this chapter drew on a memoir of the last week's events prepared on April 15, 1945, by Betty Brown and Hazel Royall Stephens of the Georgia Warm Springs Foundation staff. Betty Brown generously supplied it to the author.

# *Chronology*

*Dates of FDR Visits to Georgia, 1924-1945*

October 3 to October 20, 1924.
April 1 to May 15, 1925.
March 27 to May 5, 1926.
September 20 to November 10, 1926.
February 11 to May 12, 1927.
May 24  to June 11, 1927.
July 29 to August 3, 1927.
September 27 to December 5, 1927.
January 20 to February 11, 1928.
February 28 to May 3, 1929.
June 20, 1928.
June 30 to July 9, 1928.
September 19 to October 5, 1928.
November 8 to December 10, 1929.
April 22 to June 4, 1929.
October 3 to October 14, 1929.
November 27 to December 4, 1929.
May 1 to May 30, 1930.

November 17 to December 10, 1930.
October 1 to October 14, 1931.
November 20 to December 10, 1931.
April 30 to May 27, 1932.
October 23, 1932.
November 23 to December 6, 1932.
January 24 to February 4, 1933.
November 17 to December 6, 1933.
November 10 to December 5, 1934.
November 21 to December 8, 1935.
April 9, 1936.
March 12 to March 26, 1937.
March 23 to April 2, 1938.
August 10, 1938.
November 21 to December 4, 1938.
March 30 to April 9, 1939.
November 22 to November 29, 1939.
April 19 to April 27, 1940.
December 15, 1940.
November 29, 1941.
April 15 to April 16, 1943.
November 28 to December 17, 1944.
March 30 to April 12, 1945.

(From a draft chronology compiled for the Franklin D. Roosevelt Warm Springs Memorial Commission by James E. Curry and Rexford G. Tugwell. Provided to the author by Frank Allcorn, Jr., Executive Director of the Commission.)

# Index